LIFE AS IT WAS
1900 TO 1950
New England Reflections

York Village School, 1931
York Maine

This book is dedicated to my little granddaughter
Emma Claire Thomson
born on December 31, 1997

Many thanks to my good friends, whose ages range from 70 to 98, for sharing their memories and experiences about life in the early 1900's:

Frances Buckley
Edward Clough
Edna Mauriello
Edna McGlynn
Frederick Meier
Ralph Murray
Maxine Osgood
Connie Small
Russell Vose

"LIFE AS IT WAS 1900 to 1950" should bring an understanding and an appreciation of another time to all who read this book.

LIFE AS IT WAS
1900 - 1950
New England Reflections

By William O. Thomson

Edited by William M. Thomson

Cover painting by Ron Goyette

Photo credits to
Peter A. Moore
Portsmouth Herald
Ed Clough
Priscilla & Lois Thomson
W.P.A.

Book Format by Ann Thomson

Copyright 1999
ISBN 0-9652055-2-5

Distributed by
'Scapes Me
135 Alewive Road
Kennebunk, ME 04043

TABLE OF CONTENTS

LIFE AS IT WAS
1900 - 1950
New England Reflections

Foreword

In the following collection of memories place yourself back in the world of grandma and grandpa. You will gain an appreciation of how they survived, and a respect for the way of life they found so worthwhile and rewarding.

Between 1900 and 1950, a way of life was lived that can never be forgotten. Our ancestors have left us a legacy by the example of their simple, straightforward lifestyle. The first half of the twentieth century symbolizes a time of life that appears less complicated to us than the present. However, for our parents, grandparents, and great-grandparents, it was a time of great challenge. Through their recollections we not only share tales of struggle but of pleasure and satisfaction as well. Stirring memories about the impact of the great depression and World War II on New England towns can inspire us. Their way of life seems unbelievable, but as their stories unfold, it will seem real and remarkable. Life between 1900 and 1950 has left an indelible impression on our heritage.

World War II had an enormous bearing on American lives. A chapter in this book follows a Marine recruit from basic training to active duty. We shall always owe a deep debt of gratitude to Ed Clough and the millions of veterans like him for their dedication and sacrifice.

Entrance to Portsmouth, New Hampshire Harbor
Naval Prison and Shipyard   Circa 1941

INTRODUCTION

If you lived in New England between the years of 1900 and 1950 you would find that most people were down to earth and unique. New England people seemed to have a sense of wisdom that shone through their daily activities. This was the spirit of the common man. Over and over again, a special image has stereotyped the people of our small coastal communities. This image has created a special sentiment in the hearts of the tourists and folks who visit here. They think that our individuality, philosophy of life, and distinctness of character are old-fashioned.

Many people think our little towns are the *authorized* version of America. We have a strong historical continuity up here in New England. The past is still alive. Our folks still solve problems with hard-headed realism and common sense. The average person's philosophy, to which more of us should aspire, is one that treats everyone the same. An example of this is a local anecdote that is told over and over again. The setting is York Harbor, Maine. It seemed John, a local old-time native, was delivering the Sunday paper to one of the rich folks in town. John used his horse and wagon to make the rounds. At one of the local waterfront estates, John's horse nibbled on the shrubs as John walked up the carriage path to drop off the paper. Early one Sunday morning the owner of the property confronted John about the situation. The conversation went like this:

"John, do you know your horse is nibbling on my shrubs when you deliver the paper?"

John answered with a shrug of his shoulders.

"I guess you didn't hear me, John." The owner said. "Your horse is eating my shrubs when you walk up this path to deliver my paper. These are expensive shrubs."

Again, John just shrugged his shoulders.

"John!" the rich man replied impatiently. "Apparently you don't know who I am. I am the president of one of

New York's leading banks. I am a former judge and an advisor to the stock market. I'm on the board of directors of several major companies, and I am very active in politics."

John looked the wealthy fellow in the eye, shrugged his shoulders again and said, "Horse ate the shrubs anyway."

This story explains a lot about old-time New Englanders. These folks had a firsthand experience in living. Their old-fashioned manners, their independent, conservative, quaint, honest, witty and outspoken ways are not a myth. New England people established a tradition that has become a legend.

Life's obstacles tested our ancestors many times because they lived in the harsh New England climate. When we hear their stories, see their pictures, and in some cases, look into their weathered faces, we realize how able-bodied and tough they were. Their life might seem like an obstacle course of harsh, difficult times, but when we look back, we realize how frail and delicate life was for them and how robust and hardy they were. Our grandparents took what life offered them and made the best of it.

On January 1, 1900, a fierce snowstorm introduced the new century to New England. Intense winds blew snow into large drifts that resulted in the shutdown of the trolleys and trains. The new

century was off to a stormy start. William McKinley was President of the United States and Theodore Roosevelt, the leader of the Rough Riders in the recently won Spanish American War, was Vice President. President McKinley fell victim to an assassin's bullet two months later. Queen Victoria of England, who ascended to the throne in 1837, had just died. The British Empire was so large it boasted of a sovereignty where the "sun never sets." Ransom E. Olds produced a car that resembled a horse-less buggy and boasted of an internal combustion engine (most cars to date were steam driven). This new vehicle cost $650.00. Steel baron Andrew Carnegie had recently retired and announced that he would spend the rest of his life dispersing his money to educational and needy causes. In Topeka, Kansas, a six-foot tall stout-hearted woman named Carrie Nation was smashing up saloons. She called them hell-holes; devil's houses; infernos of lust that must go. Armed with axes and sledge hammers, she led an army of mostly women who broke down doors, smashed bottles, poured beer from kegs into gutters, and left the speakeasies and taprooms splintered and fragmented. She claimed she was carrying out the work of the Lord, and not many bartenders dared to stand up to her when she went on the rampage.

MEDICINE AND THE FAMILY DOCTOR

In Lubec, Maine on July 13, 1901, Connie Small, only nine days old, had a case of the German measles. Her mother had the disease when she delivered Connie at home. The local doctor spent a lot of time at the house caring for Connie and her mother while the illness ran its course. Two years later Connie came down with an inflammation of the lungs and Doctor Bennett actually moved into the house and stayed with her for three days until the crisis passed.

A few years later when she contracted pneumonia the only known cure was to make sure the patient had access to plenty of fresh air. Even though Connie was sick in the winter, her father took out her bedroom window to give her more air. To keep Connie warm, her mother heated bricks in the hot wood stove, wrapped them in cloth, and placed them around her in the bed Then she covered Connie with blankets. The room was so cold that her mother and father had to wear winter clothes. The medicine she took was a combination of herbs that her mother had boiled down the previous fall. Goldenrod, catnip, and rosemary were popular for cough medicine.

The sulfur bag that Connie had worn around her neck since Christmas did not prevent her pneumonia. Many kids wore these bags from December until March to fend off colds. When Connie caught a cold, her mother made an onion plaster by boiling onions, mixing them with lard, and putting the contents in a cloth bag. She applied this to Connie's chest at bedtime to loosen up congestion. Connie said, "It may have worked, but it sure had a strong smell!"

Mothers made many medical remedies at home from recipes passed down from family to family. A lot of these concoctions originated from native Americans. Our ancestors knew which barks and herb compounds, when mixed together, cured an ailment. For example, a person relieved pain by drinking a tea made from the bark of a willow tree. Although they did not know it at the time, the bark contained salicylic acid, an ingredient in today's aspirin. They used milkweed, tea, sauerkraut, gunpowder, cobwebs, frogs, birds, and sarsaparilla extensively to prepare many homemade medicines. They treated almost every kind of medical need with ointments made from herbs. Camphor oil was very popular for treating colds. They doused a flannel cloth with the oil and tied it around their neck -- what a smell! Head lice in a child's hair created a real problem. They wrapped an infected child's head in a kerosene-soaked towel for two or three days.

Another experience Connie Small remembers is that of having an earache. Her father knew what to do. He lit up his corncob pipe, inhaled the smoke, and then exhaled it into her aching ear. Warm smoke calmed her and relieved some of the pain.

People treated open cuts with Iodine, a deep reddish brown liquid. It stung when they poured it into an open wound, and it left a stain on the skin that lasted for days. If they had iodine on their hands, young girls wore gloves until the stains disappeared.

New England Doctor Mary E. Barrell

A Doctor performed tonsil operations in a patient's kitchen or dining room. He placed a cone filled with ether over the patient's nose and when the patient went under, he started the surgery. The Doctor also set broken bones in the home. Because he made so many house calls, he became part of the family. He was a counselor, psychologist, and a good friend. These town doctors performed some extraordinary medical feats and they developed long-lasting friendships with each family.

SCHOOL DAYS

In the early 1900's, most small New England towns had two schools -- an elementary school and a high school. A small two-story building with two rooms, one on each floor, served as the elementary school. Each room contained up to five different grade levels with a total of about twenty kids in the classroom. Two teachers ran the entire building. The teacher taught her grade levels one period at a time. When she worked with one grade, the other students studied, read lessons, or completed assignments. Sometimes older students tutored younger kids.

Discipline was never a problem. The teacher used a large razor strap, a ruler, and a rubber hose to punish any disorderly conduct. If a child misbehaved he stood in front of the class, held out his hands, and received a blow from the teacher's strap or ruler. She used the hose on students' legs. Occasionally, the ruler cut the child's hand and the sight of this kept the students in line, as no one wanted to be the next victim.

1931 School Days, York Village

Sometimes a student sat under the teacher's desk for a short period of time, or stood alone in a small room or hallway for as long as the teacher felt necessary. Every classroom had a dunce stool and the student sitting on the stool usually wore a tall hat with the word "dunce" printed on it. If the teacher disciplined a child at school the parents supported her, and many children received a second punishment at home. Physical discipline was common in the early 1900's.

Schools taught the difference between right and wrong and there was never any confusion about what was right, and what was wrong. Honesty, respect, responsibility, and fairness were at the top of the list. They always stressed compassion for others.

Many students walked two or more miles to school because there were no school buses. Some communities sent out a pick-up truck with benches in the back, to bring in kids who lived a great distance from the school. In the winter months they rigged canvas curtains around the truck-bed to protect the riders from the cold. The children who walked to school met their classmates on the way and they all walked together. Weather was not a deterrent. If their clothes were wet when they arrived at school, the kids went down to the boiler room and dried them by standing in front of the roaring fire.

The children often took shortcuts through fields and woods. Certain days along the coast, the wind chill was so fierce that kids walked along the shoreline to get beneath the level of the road which provided a barrier from the wind. If fresh snow was deep, an older child led the way, allowing the little kids to step in his footprints to make it easier for them to walk through the drifts. Big kids watched over little ones and made sure that they arrived at school safely. Everyone wore a stocking hat, a pair of mittens, and a scarf that a family member hand knitted.

There were no carpets in the schools. Most had wide wooden floorboards that were treated with oil every year to preserve them. These floors had their own unique smells, creeks, and squeaks. Iron or wood pegs were nailed into the wall outside the classroom to hang up outdoor clothing. The students placed their boots and overshoes on the floor directly under their coat or jacket.

Youngsters had their own individual desk. In some schools the desks and seats were screwed into the floor, while in others, they were fastened onto a small platform. Each desk had a small round hole in the top right-hand corner for a glass inkwell that the teacher filled with ink from a large bottle. Only the students in the fourth grade and higher used the inkwells. Writing in ink was very special and younger students looked forward to it. When they were ready, she gave them a black wooden pen holder with a steel point inserted at the tip. They dipped it in the well and if they weren't careful, ink went everywhere but on the paper. The students dried up any excess ink with blotters.

Most schools taught the Rinehart method of writing. Lined paper helped the students align their letters properly. In the front of each classroom, large blackboards secured to the walls displayed the alphabet with its letters perfectly formed. Good handwriting was one of the most important skills children learned and they spent many hours practicing penmanship.

Part of learning to write was learning how to hold the pen. The teacher walked up and down the aisles and pulled a pen from a child's writing hand to check for proper grasp. If she pulled the pencil easily from the writer's hand, the grip was correct. If it was hard to pull, the writer worked on holding the pencil with less firmness. They also tried to force a left-handed writer to write with the right hand. If a student used the left to write, the teacher rapped his knuckles with a book or ruler and forced him to change hands. They sincerely believed that people should only write with their right hands and penmanship experts during that time geared all of their writing instructions to right-handed writers.

Teachers taught almost every subject with a blackboard. Creative teachers drew stories with chalk that allowed an adventure to unfold before the students' eyes. They demonstrated spelling, math, and all types of written exercises on the blackboards. Drill, drill, and more drill; practice and repeat; if a student didn't get it, the teacher called on him over and over again until embarrassment forced him to understand the lesson.

Schools established dress codes and they enforced them. Girls wore either dresses or blouses and skirts. Boys wore slacks and shirts. Mothers made school clothes at home from materials that varied from store-bought, to material from empty feed bags. Grain sacks were very pretty and they were suitable for making clothes such as shirts, dresses, skirts, and slacks. It was a challenge to find enough grain sacks of the same color or print to make the clothes. Because clothes were cheaper to make than to purchase, family members sewed frequently. Dresses, pajamas, and flannel shirts were all homemade. The women repaired any damaged clothes because they knew the art of sewing, knitting, and darning. Lots of kids from large families wore hand-me-downs – folks did not throw anything away. Since girls wore dresses to school even in winter, they pulled slacks up under their dress to keep it from wrinkling. They removed the slacks at school and hung them up with their jacket.

At recess the boys played on one side of the school yard and the girls on the other side. The girls played games like tag, dodge ball, kick-the-ball, and hop scotch. The boys played football or softball. In winter the teachers banned snowballs from the play areas and if the teacher caught a student throwing them, she disciplined the child. School hours were from 9:00 to 12:00 and 1:00 to 3:00. Kids who walked to school went home for lunch. Kids who were unable to get home brought their lunch to school and ate it in the classroom. Each morning a local dairy farmer delivered small bottles of fresh milk that the children enjoyed as a mid-morning snack with crackers.

Kids always noticed the large roaring coal fire in the furnace as they descended the stairs to the bathrooms in the basement. Everyone called the bathrooms the girls' and boys' *basements*. These areas were not well lit. The stalls had very little light. It always seemed cold and dark because the only windows were small cellar windows with the glass painted gray so nobody could see into the bathrooms. Russell Vose tells a story about his teacher standing outside the doorway to the boys' room clapping her hands and admonishing the kids to do their duty and get out in a hurry.

At holiday times, regardless of the season, each class decorated their windows: pumpkins, Easter bunnies, valentines, and yes, those wonderful Christmas decorations. They proudly displayed their snowmen, angels, Christmas trees, manger scenes, and candles. Each holiday the kids had a special party with fresh ice cream that they made right in the room. Mothers sent in cupcakes or decorated cookies. During school hours, kids put on a pageant and many mothers tried to attend, bringing along younger sisters or brothers. The children in each class had their own little orchestra that included tambourines, a metal triangle hit with a stick, and a drum. The teacher played the old upright piano -- didn't those kids sing! It was great fun.

One of the few unpleasant memories was the day when the school doctor arrived to vaccinate the students, at no charge.

That was a horrible experience. The boys tried not to cry as the doctor punched that large needle into their arm. It was a traumatic time for all of the kids. The

School Children

school dentist also came to school and if a student's teeth did not measure up, he gave him a note for his parents advising them of the problems.

Families dreaded diseases such as measles, mumps, whooping cough, and small pox. If a student came down with scarlet fever the family's house was quarantined. A health official posted a sign on the front door and from that date until cured, only family members entered the house. Polio was the most feared illness at that time, and people prayed that this disease did not hit their family. Polio left some students permanently crippled.

Elementary teachers were all single women. The first time a student had a male teacher might be in the eighth grade. Elementary school principals were also women. In small towns, women teachers attended the same local church as their students and they often rented rooms from a student's family, making it difficult for the kids to avoid their teacher. When the teacher was near, everyone was on their best behavior.

In 1940, Frances Buckley taught in a two-room schoolhouse in the town of Beebe River, just north of Plymouth, New Hampshire. Frances was the acting principal as well as the fifth through eighth grade teacher. She supervised the teacher who taught grades one through four in the other schoolroom. Both teachers lived in a local boarding house. They each paid $7.00 per week rent, which included delicious home-cooked meals. Frances earned a salary of $90.00 per month, or $850.00 per year since she received no pay for vacations. Most of the students' parents worked in the local mill owned by the Draper Corporation.

Frances taught five children in the fifth grade, three in the sixth, four in the seventh, and five in the eighth, for a total of seventeen students. She grouped the grades by level. Each grade sat in their own row and had their own textbooks. Books used by more than one grade, such as science and history, were shared. When she taught spelling, she gave the fifth graders their first word, then the sixth graders received their first word. She gave each grade a more difficult word than the previous grade, until each level mastered their own ten words. When Frances taught math to one grade, she put assignments on a blackboard for the other grades to practice until she could spend time with them. Each grade worked independently from the others. Every youngster focused on their own grade level work.

A wood stove located in the basement provided heat. A high school student brought the wood in early every morning, cleaned out the ashes and started the fire. The wood burned all day and the building stayed warm. He repeated the process in the late afternoon.

In the winter months during a fifteen minute recess break, the kids tobogganed down a steep slope in the yard behind the school. Frances went sliding with them and when the fifteen minutes were up, she rang a cow bell and the kids all scrambled back to class. Recess occurred twice a day, morning and afternoon. At noon the students were dismissed for a one and one-half hour lunch break. Children hurried home and started to prepare a hot meal for themselves and their parents, who had a one hour break from the mill. Elementary kids did not have homework. After school, kids did their chores at home and played. Everyone had something to do. This was a time when youngsters experienced the joys and wonders of life.

Teachers were very proper and took their role seriously, as the following story illustrates. In 1927, Fred Meier went on the annual Wellesley High School trip to New York city. President Calvin Coolidge was staying on the first floor of the hotel and Fred's class was on the 11th floor. Also staying at the hotel, on the 22nd floor, was world heavyweight boxer Gene Tunney, who had just defeated Jack Dempsey. Fred's teacher arranged for the class to attend a reception for President Coolidge. The class left the 11th floor and when the elevator arrived on the first floor Fred Meier stayed behind. He went up to Gene Tunney's floor where he met the champ. Tunney was very friendly and cordial and even put his arm around Fred. When Fred returned to his class, President Coolidge had already left. The fact that he had chosen to meet Tunney rather than the President outraged his teacher. She gave him a stern lecture, telling him that he was unpatriotic for seeing a boxing champion rather than the President of the United States. To reinforce her views, she failed Fred in his next exam. She told him that she feared that he wanted to be a big-league ballplayer or a heavyweight fighter and that these were not respectable goals. If she had seen into the future, she would have realized that Fred later served in the United States Air Force during World War II, spent twenty-nine months overseas, and completed nine combat missions. When he returned home after the service, he earned a doctorate, became a college president, and before he retired, he received three honorary doctorates. Small schools and dedicated teachers turned out great people.

FAMILY LIFE

In the first part of the twentieth century, students learned proper manners in school and at home. Kids did not listen to conversations between adults unless the adults invited them to participate. They addressed Uncles and Aunts as *Uncle* and *Aunt* and neighbors as *Mr.*, *Mrs.*, and *Miss*. Children did not chew gum or use profanity. Sure, boys might let loose in the barn or in a field, but not when adults were within earshot. If a young boy took a puff on an acorn pipe or tried to roll a cigarette, chances are he was a good mile into the woods and he posted a guard to make sure he wasn't followed. Father's word was law and a child never questioned him. When dad spoke and asked to have something done, the child followed his orders immediately.

Charles Steward Homestead

Before the invention of the automobile, horse-and-buggies provided most of the transportation. Families that ran a business that depended upon transportation usually owned their own wagons. If a family did not have a horse and wagon they hired one from a local stable or farm. They used buckboards to go on trips. Local townspeople walked everywhere. Around 1911, the first few cars appeared on the streets and they scared more than a few horses. Usually a local person had a car for hire and on special occasions a family rented a vehicle. Gas stations pooped-up in each town as cars became more popular.

If a family was lucky, they had one car. The man of the house always drove the vehicle. Most automobiles in the 1920's and 30's had a three-speed clutch shift. Dad worried about the radiator freezing in the winter or boiling over in the summer. Most roads were dirt or gravel and turning wheels bounced stones off the underside of the car causing a loud ping. Stones also cut into tires and caused flats that dad changed on the spot. If the spare tire went flat he drove the car home on the rim. This was a long slow rough drive and the driver's disposition wasn't too pleasant. Cars backfired when the motor misfired and created a small explosion that sounded like a gun firing. In some cars, the backfire lasted for several minutes until the driver adjusted the spark control. A long trip was a nerve-racking experience.

On a family trip all the kids piled in, some sat on others' laps. Father always drove and Mother always sat in the front. Seat belts were unheard-of and dad stopped frequently and shifted the children's seating. The upholstery was made from coarse cloth and the windows rolled up and down by turning the crank attached to the door. The heater was a small rig suspended in front of the right front passenger seat. Long, distant rides were very tiring, especially when the whole family went along. Gas sold for about twenty cents a gallon. Each town had one or two gas stations that serviced cars. The local owner of the station greased and oiled the cars, and made repairs when necessary. However, when the mechanic lifted the hood and looked under it, he always saw the owner looking in from the other side to supervise the job.

By 1926, one in six citizens owned a car. Edna McGlynn said that her father called his 1917 Ford his *one extravagance*. He declared that if his father had a horse, then he could have a car. Cars were costly and some folks felt that they were unduly lavish. Maxine

Osgood had another problem. Her dad drove a 1926 touring car and he chewed tobacco. She rode in the back seat behind him. She said, "You can bet I never went for a ride with the back window open!"

Josiah Norton Farm
Josiah Norton, Chester Norton, Alice Caswell, Helen Norton

Since most women did not drive, dad drove mom to town on Saturday so she could do errands. Mom shopped in the store and bought one week's supply of food for less than twelve dollars. Oatmeal was a staple item, usually cooked in a double boiler at night, and left on the stove for breakfast. Cream-of-Wheat was also a popular breakfast cereal. Lots of milk and homemade toast topped off breakfast. The general meal consisted of good stews, meat, potatoes, and vegetables. Lunch was usually soup and sandwiches. Grandma made the best vanilla-frosted chocolate cake , and she kept the cakes coming.

Shopping for groceries was an interesting experience. A family with a phone called in their order and the store delivered it at no charge. Mom-and-pop neighborhood varieties were everywhere. A good sized store was only as large as a one story house. Sawdust covered the store floors, a cat always patrolled the premises (mouse control), and the shopkeepers sold the cheese, butter, and bacon in slabs. They ground the fresh-cut meat themselves, and kept a full pickle barrel near the meat counter. The owners stocked items in high piles around the outside walls and the shelves reached to the ceilings. They placed can goods, glassware, and heavy items on the bottom shelves and paper products and soft goods on the top. If a customer wanted an item from the top shelf, the grocer took a long

Nelson C. Hutchins Store
Nelson C. Hutchins, Proprietor, Cape Neddick Maine

round pole, poked the item up into the air, and caught it as it fell.

Sometimes the grocer used a sliding ladder suspended on pulleys attached to the top shelf to retrieve heavier items or to restock.

The grocers wore a straw hat and had a pencil parked behind an ear. They wrote the price of each purchased item on the side of a brown paper bag and added the figures in their head. Mom paid the bill, and the grocer packed up the order in the paper bag. If the store was within walking distance, one of the children came along and pulled the groceries home in a wood-sided wagon.

The kids liked to buy penny candy. Five cents purchased a considerable amount because some candies only cost five-for-a-penny. A large assortment of brightly colored candy filled a glass display case. The youngsters took their time making their final decisions and tested the duration of the clerk's patience. The grocers personally knew each family member and they treated their customers as if they were part of their own family. They gave credit to their customers who then paid their bills either weekly or monthly. During hard times, the grocer sometimes extended credit terms for a needy family.

Everyone in the neighborhood knew their neighbors and they showed compassion when a family was in need. The closeness of the families kept the kids in line. It was like having parents in each house. Adults spoke up when a child did something wrong, even if it was not their child. Later they relayed the event to the child's parents. No one took offense if someone else corrected their child because the basic standards of right and wrong applied to everyone.

Most family homes built between 1900 and 1950 were typical New England homes or cottages. They consisted of a living room, dining room, and a kitchen with a walk-in pantry on the first floor. Three bedrooms and a bath made up the second floor. A full basement housed a storage area and the coal burning furnace that provided heat. Coal was delivered by a large open dump truck and was stored in a coal bin in the cellar. A chute ran from the truck to an open cellar window located over the coal bin and the driver dumped the coal down the chute into the bin below. Although dusty at times, it was fun to watch the coal bouncing noisily down the metal slide.

The pantry or kitchen had a soapstone sink and plenty of cabinets for storing pots and pans. Mother prepared the family meals on a large black iron stove. One section of the stove contained an area for the fire that helped heat the kitchen. Other

Cottage Circa 1938

compartments provided areas of different heat levels for different types of cooking. It's amazing that Mom could regulate the heat for baking, and nothing ever burned. She also heated water on the stove for washing, cleaning, and baths. The stove heated irons for ironing clothes and curling-irons for curling hair.

A steam radiator in each first-floor room in the house heated both floors. The radiators varied in size depending upon the size of the room. Every once in a while a radiator popped and whistled when the pressure valve released some excess vapor. On cold mornings beautiful patterns of frost covered the glass window behind the radiator. Everyone believed that Jack Frost drew the pictures and kids couldn't resist drawing on the frozen steamed windows with their fingers. On real cold days, dad hung heavy curtains at the bottom of the stairs to contain the heat. Most homes did not have radiators installed in the second floor rooms. Instead, heat rose up from the downstairs rooms through heat grates cut into the upstairs floors. The central furnace in the basement chugged along at a good pace and the men tended the fire and kept the furnace clean. Every night dad banked the fire so it would burn until the morning.

The houses contained basic furnishings. In most living rooms a Morris chair occupied the place of prominence where dad or pa always sat, across from the upright piano in the corner. A large oak dining room table with matching chairs and sideboard, dominated most dining rooms. The kitchen table had a tin-top, ideal for activities such as preparing food, eating, or playing family games. The bathroom had a large white porcelain bathtub with claw feet. It was used once a week for the Saturday night bath. The pedestal wash basin matched the tub.

In most small New England towns, families maintained a garden and kept animals for food such as horses, pigs, cows, and chickens. The animals and garden needed a lot of care, so each youngster had many chores. This was part of the self-sufficient survival chain that sustained many families. Girls went down to the shore and gathered sea moss when mom made Belomonge or seaweed pudding. Apple pie made from apples grown in one's own yard tasted great and fresh-baked johnnycake (yellow corn bread) was delicious served warm. Girls' chores were done inside the home and boys' chores were done outside the home. Despite the work, there was still time to skate, slide, or play some type of game.

Some homes were really mini farms. From 1918 to 1925, Fred Meier lived on a small farm with over one hundred hens, a cow, and a horse. Fred claims he learned a great deal about life and survival. He plowed furrows, spliced lines, harnessed the horse, and milked the cow. Each family member learned responsibility. Farm work was endless but rewarding when the results of the hard labor appeared on the table. Farmers adjusted to challenges with common sense and straightforward thinking.

Once a week people gathered at the town hall to watch a movie for a five-cent admission price. During a silent movie a local person played the piano, keeping pace with the action on the screen. Edna McGlynn went to the movies on Friday night or Saturday afternoon. Two of the most popular films were *The Perils of*

Pauline starring Pearl White, and *The Goddess* with Anita Stewart. These were both serials. Each week the episode ended with Pauline or the Goddess in a perilous situation and with the viewers wondering if she would escape. Everyone went back the following week to find out what happened. The damsel in distress escaped every week, but another crisis inevitably developed before the end of the new episode, which prompted the audience to return again to see what happened. The series went on and on, and people loved it. Popcorn was a standard refreshment and five cents purchased a large box. The brightly colored portable popcorn machine stood ready to move to the sidewalk for a town parade. Dances were also held in the town hall and square dancing was popular. Dance instruction studios taught anyone, including young children, the ballroom dancing steps.

Because most housewives didn't drive, vendors brought their wares to the homes. Horse-drawn wagons delivered vegetables, ice, milk, and fish. Rag men, garbage men, and scissors' grinders also made the rounds.

A wooden ice box kept food from spoiling. A piece of ice in the top of the box kept the food cold. As the ice melted, water ran through a tube and into a pan placed under the box. The pan was emptied often or it overflowed and soaked the floor. When she

John E. Bridges & Son ICE, York Maine

-26-

needed ice, the woman of the house placed a colored card in her window. The color indicated the size piece of ice needed. The ice man saw the card and chipped a chunk of ice from the large block in the back of his sawdust covered wagon. He picked up the ice with a pair of tongs and slung the block up over his shoulder which he covered with a rubber apron. He carried it to the customer's ice box and placed it inside. The size of the piece determined the price.

The vegetable man owned his own farm and during the summer seasons he offered fresh vegetables for sale two or three times a week. Some of the men exhibited a sense of humor when they tried to sell fresh cucumbers for eight cents each or three for a quarter. The rag man purchased rags and junk, and the garbage man collected table scraps for his pig farm. Some towns even had a soap man who made the rounds selling soap. Fred Meier likes to tell a story about one door-to-door soap man who was good at public relations and full of good stories. He ran his hands over a child's head and said something complimentary to the child's mother, claiming to read fortunes by the shape of the head. When he felt Fred's head, he ran his fingers over a couple of bumps and said, "This kid doesn't have too much on the ball -- but he's going to be awful lucky!"

The milkman delivered glass bottles of fresh milk once or twice a week. On cold mornings the milk froze and the cream popped off the bottle cap, and rose four or five inches above the top of the bottle. Mom cut off the cream, thawed it, and served it with desserts. Some of the milkmen also delivered eggs and butter.

The scissors grinder sharpened knives, scissors, and small tools. He usually rode a bicycle and his grinding equipment hooked up to the wheels. To sharpen something he jacked up the wheel and peddled the bike, spinning the wheel that powered the grinding stone.

During the first half of the century, families were fairly large. Most marriages produced a child within the first year. The next child could be born about two years later. This pace continued until the mother could not have any more children. It was not uncommon to have as many as ten children in one family. If a child was born into too large a family, the financial burden of caring for another baby might be too much, and one of the children could be raised by a relative. Sometimes this was a permanent situation and sometimes the child returned to his own family if they were in a position to take care of him.

The life expectancy of a child was much lower during the child's first ten years. Diphtheria and small pox claimed many young lives. A mother with seven living children might have delivered nine. New England graveyards are filled with tiny stones that mark the deaths of small infants.

OCCUPATIONS

The way people made livings shaped the economic, social, and political structure of the town.. Fishing, working in cotton and woolen mills, and   factory work all shaped   New Englanders' lifestyles.

David W. Young, First Rural Mail Carrier
York Maine, Circa 1920

Fishing

In many of the small coastal towns the principal occupation was fishing. In the northern coastal towns, the sardine business was the major industry, and many sardine processing plants were in full operation. When a whistle blew notifying the locals that a fishing boat docked with a catch of small herring, kids and adults ran down to the factory to start the process of packing. Families worked side by side processing the fish. After they cut off the heads and tails, they arranged six sardines in each small can. The fish were packed in oil or mustard and they were quite tasty. Then they placed tops on the cans, sealed them, and packed the cans in cartons for immediate shipment. During the busy season, a large surrey with double horses went out early every morning and picked up workers who lived several miles away. They brought them back home at the end of the day.

If residents in one of these towns did not pack sardines, they probably worked in a smoked herring factory. There, workers removed fish skin and cut off the heads and tails to prepare the fish for smoking. After the smoking process, they packed them in wooden boxes, about the size of a shoe box. The workers nailed the boxes shut and shipped them out to warehouses for distribution to larger cities.

In 1900, the state of Maine was the only producer of canned sardines in the United States. The industry was very seasonal. In the small coastal towns of northern Maine, entire families worked in the sardine business. Fathers, mothers, children, cousins, aunts, uncles, and grandparents worked together in these factories. In 1910, seventy-five sardine factories operated in the state. Maine exempted children from the early child labor laws because these kids worked with perishable goods. Many young children were cutters. Just think of the potential danger here. Some kids stood on platforms just to reach the cutting benches. Oily fish debris that accumulated during the processing covered the wet slippery floors. Some of these kids worked with sharp knives for ten straight hours a day, sixty hours in a week. Even a small finger cut caused great pain when it came in contact with the brine. Up to two hundred children, age fourteen and less, worked in these factories at any one time.

The industry created a social problem in the area of education. Working children only attended schools when the factories were closed, and the kids forced to work were not properly educated. The money children earned helped the family during the off-season when logging, fishing, boat building, or some farming provided a limited income. An entire family generated an income of about $35.00 per week during canning season. In 1911, Maine passed legislation regulating the working requirements for children which put the kids back into the schools. Some communities tried to schedule school hours around the seasons, giving students time off during certain months so a youngster could work in a seasonal occupation such as farming or fishing. Many students graduated from high school at the age of twenty, since it could take six or more years to finish the requirements because of work interruptions. It was also not uncommon to find a few twenty year olds playing on a high school athletic team.

Fish Pier

Making a living as a fisherman was one of the most difficult ways to earn money. Thick fog, heavy seas, mending nets, repairing traps and the uncertainty of the daily market price of fish and lobster, all added up to a feast or famine existence. Cod, haddock, mackerel, lobster, and herring, were just a few of the fish found in New England waters.

The lobster man usually made his own boat and fished by himself. His boat was his partner as their survival depended upon each other. He always referred to his boat as "she" even if it carried a male name. The affection and relationship between man and boat were magical. A lobster man's house was easy to spot because traps, buoys, and ropes filled his yard. He hauled his traps one by one, and sold the lobsters to a local distributor within hours of the catch.

Lobster Cove, York Harbor
Fiddler Foss and Grover Perkins

If a fisherman lived in one of the larger cities, he worked on a larger boat. These boats fished at the Georges Bank, about 200 miles out, and some went to the Grand Banks, about 1100 miles out to sea. The dangers faced by fishermen then, were as perilous as those faced by today's fishermen. Storms blew in without notice and massive waves tossed the small boats around with exceptional violence. Boats strained their creaking joints as the captains tried to steer a course and surge ahead. Nature tormented the fishermen. Their shear courage, strength of mind, and physical endurance conquered the elements. They were almost fearless and they had plenty of guts and grit.

Lobster Man

Salt fishing was common at the beginning of the twentieth century. A schooner sailed many miles out to sea and when it reached the fishing grounds, the crew lowered dories over the side. Each dory held two fishermen who fished with hand lines and hooks. When they filled the dory with fish, the men rowed back to the schooner and unloaded their catch. They not only caught the fish, they cut, gutted, and cleaned them. Then they salted them and let them dry. Salting preserved the fish because refrigeration was not available.

By 1920, power boats replaced the dory method of fishing. This was the beginning of net fishing. In the late1920's, the port of Gloucester, Massachusetts had over two hundred fishing boats bringing in catches totaling over two million pounds of fish a day. There were two types of boats, *long trippers* and *day trippers*. A long tripper went to sea for several days or a few weeks at a time. Day trippers sailed out in the morning and returned the same day.

Lets take a look at the day tripper. The skipper woke up long before dawn, around 3:00 a.m., to check the weather. Weather was crucial and if he felt that conditions were not favorable, he would not sail. The four-man crew showed up at 4:00 a.m. to begin the day's work. Many boats were family owned and fathers, sons, uncles and nephews made up many crews. The men of an entire family could be wiped out if one of these boats went down in a disaster. Next, the crew put ice on board and made the ship ready to sail. As the skipper sailed his ship out of the harbor, the rest of the crew prepared the nets and got the pen boards and boxes ready for the day's haul. A pen board separated the fish in the hold. They used the boxes to pack the different kinds of fish. The boxes were two-feet wide by four-feet long and when packed with ice, each weighed approximately 150 pounds.

When they spotted a school of fish, the crew dropped the net while the skipper maneuvered the boat so the net encircled the school. They secured the net and then hauled it up with a heavy winch. When they released it, the catch of fish toppled onto the deck. The crew shoveled the fish into the hold and two or three men sorted them into the proper pens and boxes. The rest of the men washed the slimy fish scales off the slippery deck. If a fisherman slipped and fell, he could be lost overboard or break an arm, wrist, or leg. The men who packed the fish watched out for rusty nails and sharp edges that could cause cuts and fatal infections such as tetanus.

When the ship sailed home, each box was tagged with the type of fish inside. The crew then cleaned the equipment and began to make the ship ready for the following day. After docking, they lowered a hook from the pier into the hold. The men placed straps around the boxes, attached them to the hook and slowly hoisted each box up to the pier. They repeated this until the hold was empty. They loaded the boxes onto a truck, ready for delivery to the local market. Finally the crew carried empty pen boxes back on board for the next day's journey. At about 6:00 p.m. they finished their work.

The skipper kept an accurate record of the types and weights of fish caught that day. He did this on a daily basis because the price of fish fluctuated every day. He charged expenses to the boat. Every Friday the skipper divided the weekly profits (called shares) and distributed the money to the men. Some of the men's wives waited at the pier to take the cash for household expenses, before their husbands drank away the profits at the local pub. Each wife usually gave her husband a small allotment that he could use to buy his drinks. The men did not fish on Friday.

Fishermen were very superstitious. Sailing on a Friday was considered unlucky. If a hawk or crow came to rest in the rigging, the fishermen felt that an omen of bad luck had just descended onto their ship. They always filled buckets completely to the top and never left them half-full. They were careful to never drop a hatch into a hold. A half-full bucket or a dropped hatch brought bad luck. Most ship captains carried a horseshoe on board and they nailed it upside down over the cabin door to catch any sinister signs or tokens of bad luck.

Young fishermen always looked after and respected the older fishermen. Younger men bought the old salts drinks and often invited the old men to their homes for a meal. Dinner consisted of fish chowder, lobster, fried squid, and many other delicious sea items that came up with the nets. The women called these *sea harvest* dinners. There was also a charity box on every pier, placed in an inconspicuous location. It contained fresh fish for the old salts, so they would always have a meal.

Old salts taught *sailors' sense* to the younger men. Sailors' sense is the ability to read the sea, the wind, the sky, the sun, and the clouds. It is the ability to analyze the sounds of the ship as it plows through the waves. Sailors know what mother nature is telling them. They know how to read these signs and understand how the different elements blend together. This extra sense gives the men an awareness of what possible dangers lie ahead.

These fishermen had a great respect for the forces of nature and a great respect for their mentors, the "Old Salts" who taught them the ways of fishing. Many fishermen were lost at sea, others fought hardships and tragedies, but this was part of the lifestyle for the brave men who chose to follow the sea. In the fishing town of Gloucester, Massachusetts, a fishermen's memorial statue represents over ten thousand men who have lost their lives to the sea.

Mills

Many small New England towns were established around some type of mill. If it wasn't a cotton mill it was a lumber mill, paper mill, or a shoe shop. The particular industry defined the lifestyles and politics of the town's residents. The people knew no other way of life than the life of the mill.

In the small town of Beebe River, New Hampshire, the parents of Frances Buckley's students made wooden bobbins at the Draper Corporation. The large cotton mills throughout New England used these bobbins, or spindles, to dispense thread as it was woven into sheets. The mill corporation owned most of the houses in Beebe River. Families paid small rents, and the mill maintained the property. Every other year a painter would paint the exteriors of the homes and the next year he painted the interiors. The town had two telephones, a public telephone in the boarding house, and a private phone in the mill manager's house. When the manager and his family were away, they left their doors unlocked so that any person who needed to make a local call, could walk in and use the phone. Everyone trusted each other.

A horn or whistle defined and regulated a mill worker's day. Mills controlled schedules. The first whistle sounded at 6:00 a.m. to alert workers that the mill opened in one hour. Most workers had been up since 5:00 a.m. getting ready to go to work. For a working housewife, the day was long and tiring. She had to care for a family in addition to getting herself ready for work. She had to feed the kids, pack lunches, and get children to a baby-sitter before 6:30 a.m.

She then raced off to her job. The whistle blew at noon to announce the beginning of lunch hour, and again at 1:00p.m. when lunch hour ended. The last whistle at 5:00 p.m. signaled the end of the work day. She picked up the children, and probably stopped at the local market for groceries, before returning home to cook the evening meal for the entire family. House chores followed this long and tedious day. Caring for the family was not part of a man's responsibility.

The conditions at cotton mills were difficult, dirty and unpleasant. The air was contaminated with fine pieces of lint, dust and dirt. The workers wore handkerchiefs over their noses and mouths for protection against inhaling the dangerous contaminants. By the end of the workday the white handkerchiefs had turned black. Every night the workers soaked, washed, and dried, the handkerchiefs to get them ready for the next day. Tuberculosis, a disease faced by many workers, was known as *white death*. Many towns had TB hospitals that cared for patients who came down with the dreaded disease. Mill windows were never opened and inside temperatures could reach as high as 106-degrees. This is why they were known as *sweat shops* and why many workers suffered from lung and heart related illnesses. Many mill owners did not observe child labor laws. It wasn't until 1938 that strict regulations were put in place. Before then, during inspections, young workers were hidden in bathrooms, out of sight.

Labor unions started to organize just after 1910. Workers were expected to work on holidays for regular wages -- no overtime. They were at the mercy of their boss. They were forced to take wage cuts if demand or production fell. Some mill owners took advantage of workers, expecting them to work long hours under brutal conditions. If they complained they were fired. Every day the worker faced foul smells and a factory filled with loud noise. Pounding machines shook buildings and deafened ears. It was scary for many young workers.

Safety equipment was minimal and in many cases it did not exist. Nuts or bolts flew off machines and brackets let go. Flying pieces of material or machinery knocked out teeth and cut or bruised many workers. Some employees, including children, were scalped when their hair was caught and tangled in a powerful machine. The foreman was more interested in the damage to the machine than he was in the worker's injury. Employees were rapidly replaced. The foreman told the injured workers to "get cured and get back on the job, as fast as possible." The mill policy was no pay for no production. In some cases, an unconscious worker was carried home and left there with no career and no income.

Machines with blades cut off the ends of fingers. Machines that grabbed and pulled materials caught workers' arms and legs. In shoe shops the splinters, buffers, shavers, stackers, and ringers pounded noisily in competition with each other. Jobs were so monotonous that workers screamed and hollered every once in a while just to ease the tension building up in their bodies. The same job repeated over and over for eight straight hours almost drove them insane. Some workers hauled hides and skins on their backs, up six flights of stairs. Unskilled laborers earned little and worked hard but they had no options. The mill offered the only jobs in town. Everyone had the ambition to move from an entry level job to a skilled position (and a larger pay check) but most mill jobs were dead end. In 1910 the average mill worker earned between $5.00 and $8.00 per week.

Mills expanded, and immigrants moved into the towns and cities to find employment.. Greeks, Armenians, Portuguese, Italian, Irish, Scottish, French, Turkish and many other ethnic families worked together side by side. After work, the men stopped by the local pub for a five-cent beer. They talked, found common interests, and developed a respect for each other. Everyone in the community knew everyone else and the community became close. Mill athletic teams organized and the competition was fierce. Mill families supported the teams by attending weekend games. Small wages barely supported their families, but the hardship brought the workers together as they struggled to survive. Despite the near-poverty and the difficult conditions, these proud folks built strong, loving families with strong values.

Factories

Most workers could not afford a car, so a weekend day meant a picnic at the local park. Large families gathered together for homemade sandwiches and drinks. Everybody had a great time. Relatives, neighbors, and friends joined in for a day of good food and fun. Local politicians showed up and gave speeches from the back of a truck or from the local bandstand. They realized the voting power of the working people and knew that workers' votes could control a local election.

Some of the workers labored in small shops where they felt wanted and more like individuals, not numbers. In fairness to large mill owners, some made it their business to know their workers, and tried to care for their families during hard times. A family might receive a food basket, blankets, or even have their rent paid by a kind owner.

In the early 1900's, Edna McGlynn's dad worked for the United Shoe Machinery Corporation in Beverly, Massachusetts.

This company was rated as one the three best production facilities in the United States. It was a well-organized company and one of the large companies that did provide for their workers. They paid slightly higher wages than factories in the surrounding area. The company built a golf course and tennis courts for their workers' enjoyment. They maintained a large skating pond in the winter. In the summer months a worker's child could caddie at the golf course or work at the tennis courts to earn a few dollars. For $1.00 per year workers' children were allowed to use these recreational facilities. Each day special trains ran from Boston to Newburyport and picked up workers who lived along the train stops. The factory had its own train station.

The company maintained a small hospital on the factory grounds that they staffed with full-time doctors and nurses. Industrial accidents were treated on the premises and the medical staff was always available for the workers' needs. When employees reached twenty-five years of service the company recognized them at a special dinner, gave them a   pin and shares of the company's stock. The United Shoe rarely laid-off anyone. Even during the depression, they kept the workers working, although they had to cut their hours to three days a week -- but at least the workers had income.

The United Shoe Company built the machines that manufactured shoes throughout the world. The company held the patents on all of the machines it manufactured and leased its machines to their customers, making United Shoe a unique and highly profitable company. It was a fine company to work for, and up until 1950, at least one member of almost every Beverly family worked for the company.

If local mills were involved in producing woolen material, paper, shoes, or fish processing, the smell from the factories never left the town. Odors permeated the air and the foul smell clung to the workers' clothes and hair. The smell in paper producing towns was particularly foul. Other mills had their own original unpleasant smells. There was no way to escape the smell of the mills. People working and living in these areas were immune to the odors and only strangers passing through town noticed. When a visitor asked, "How do you stand the smell?" the local reply was, "What smell?"

Most mill workers lived within walking distance of the mills where they worked. Apartment houses had been built row after row, on street after street around the mill. These homes did not have much land. Only the width of a driveway separated them. The average house was built either two or three floors high and was referred to as a *double decker* or *triple decker*. Each floor was built for one family. On the outside of each house, back or side porches were connected one above the other. Access to the apartments was through the side or back porches. The single front door of these homes led into a large elaborate hall that served as a front entrance to the apartment for special occasions. The average apartment consisted of a shed, two bedrooms, a kitchen, pantry, bath, living room, and dining room.

Housing

People used their porches for relaxing and sitting, and for trying to get a breath of fresh air on hot summer nights. On Monday, washday, the laundry was hung out to dry on the porch after each piece of clothing had been washed in a washing machine that had a hand operated ringer. A clothesline was created by running a rope through a pulley from the porch to another mounted on a nearby tree or pole. The laundry was hung out to dry by reeling the line back and forth. It was quite a sight to see all of this laundry flapping in the breeze. In the winter months, frozen-stiff clothes were taken off the line and thawed out on racks next to a stove or radiator. These clothes always had a fresh clean smell.

Mill families were proud of their triple decker dwellings and wives and daughters kept the houses immaculate. A landlord usually lived in one of the apartments and kept the property painted and repaired. In some of the apartments the third floor was much smaller because the roof line cut into the rooms. These were called *attic apartments* because they had slanted ceilings. Many an aunt or a grandmother and grandfather lived up in this area.

When Labor Unions organized in the early 1900's, several bloody strikes followed when workers tried to improve working conditions. These dramatic times brought death, destruction, and turmoil to the mills. In the 1920's and 30's storms, floods, and the depression closed many of the mills. Some small growth occurred during World War II from 1941 to 1945, but this was just a brief revival during the war period.

Our ancestors had to work hard in the pursuit of their dreams to make better lives for their families. They did not have much choice in their occupation because available work was determined by the industry or the location of their town. Mills and fishing were a way of life and it was almost taken for granted that the kids would follow in their parents' occupations. The common folks who worked in these jobs, had made a life for themselves. Through their efforts they enabled their children to pursue education, professions, and opportunities that had not been available to them.

FUN AND RECREATION

Between the years 1900 and 1950, most recreation was self motivated. Leisure activities revolved around schools, churches, and each individual. Basketball was a popular activity. Some schools organized teams from the elementary grades through high school. Before 1930, the practice area for this winter team sport was usually an outdoor gravel court that had to be shoveled by the players. Games were played indoors against a few local neighboring schools, at the town hall or Grange building. Halls were wrapped in fish nets to keep the ball from breaking windows or knocking down pictures. Shots were sent up over rafters and beams that were in the way. If the shot cleared the beam and went through the net, two points were scored. Some shots were called line drives because the ceilings were so low the ball had to be drilled at the basket.

York High School Girls Basketball 1911

The average playing area was small. One player said he could almost tap the ball through the hoop from the center jump position. Wood burning stoves were a hazard. Most stoves were located at the end of the playing court and a fast cut to the basket might result in a disruption of the stove and a burned player. When a wild pass knocked out the stove pipes, spectators and coaches scrambled to replace the pipes and contain the smoke.

In the 1920's an away high school game, just fifteen miles to the next town, was an overnight stay. Most roads were not plowed properly because very few automated plows existed. Snow was packed down by snow rollers drawn by a team of four to six horses. If a trolley or train was available, the team used public transportation. Many times the coach or high school principal drove the team in his private car.

Small towns played six man football. When the total population of a high school was approximately sixty students (fifteen to twenty in a class), it was difficult to field a team of just eight players. A team had 6 starters and 2 backups. Because the equipment consisted of crude, inferior padding and helmets, injuries were common and some were serious.

Baseball was also a very popular sport, not only in schools but in the towns themselves. Some small towns had an organized semi-professional team that played a weekend game on the local field. These teams were made up of college kids home for the summer and a few local former high school athletes. A game brought out a good sized crowd and it was not unusual for a small collection to be taken up to help defray the costs.

Band concerts were very popular. Local and visiting bands performed in the town's small gazebo bandstand. Local singers, some good and some bad, added to the program. When a number was finished, car horns tooted and a resounding applause showed appreciation, if not for the quality, at least for the effort. Bowling, pool, and dancing were also forms of recreation. Carnivals, the circus, special dances, church picnics and suppers, also drew good sized crowds.

Holidays were an important part of recreation. Most towns celebrated them in much the same way. On the first day of May, people celebrated *May Day*, the day to express love. They spent hours making May baskets in preparation for the day's activities. They used small paper cups or oatmeal boxes decorated with colorful paper, flowers and a handle. They filled the baskets with homemade candy and cookies, and gave them to loved ones, older people, family members, and special boyfriends or girlfriends. After a young lady left a basket on her boyfriend's steps she rang the bell and ran. If the boyfriend caught her, she received a kiss. Many times the boyfriend was more interested in the contents of the basket than the young lady who had left it. The annual May Day parade included a contest for the best decorated bicycles and doll carriages. The townspeople erected a May Pole on the front lawn of the school and young children danced around it while each held a different colored crepe paper streamer. The woven pattern of assorted bright colors that resulted created a festive atmosphere in the crowd.

The Fourth of July was another very special recreational day. To celebrate this patriotic day, people decorated their homes and businesses with red, white, and blue banners. They ate the traditional dinner -- salmon and peas. They attended the morning parade, afternoon band concert, and evening bonfire each year, and topped it all off by watching the glorious overhead fireworks display. Folks assembled the bonfire from old railroad ties for days in advance. An old wooden barrel sat on top of the twenty-foot high structure and everyone hoped that the kids wouldn't torch the pile before the scheduled time. Sometimes they posted guards to make sure this didn't happen.

One thing that made the Fourth of July different from today, was that people could purchase fireworks for their individual use. Every family bought salutes, rockets, and small bombs. Most families purchased sky rockets to set off in their yards after dark. Little kids lit sparklers and banged caps. The streets came alive with the bright flashes and loud bangs from the explosions, and the smell of burned powder filled the air. Boys tossed salutes (small fire crackers) at the girls and scared them half to death. When ignited, five-inch salutes created a huge bang. This was a dangerous practice and many times a situation could get out of control. When a salute was lit, it was often tossed away rapidly without thought of where it might land. Consequently, people were hurt, property was damaged, and fires were started.

Circus comes to town 1937

May Day   Circa 1934

Fourth of July Parade Circa 1915

The young folks looked forward to celebrating Halloween because their parents granted them permission to stay out after dark. The nighttime revelry usually led to playing a few pranks -- and pranks they played. Store windows received a good waxing either with soap or candle wax. Soap could be washed off, but wax created a problem since it was more difficult to remove. They grabbed the extra set of keys to the church from the not-so-secret hiding place and pulled the bell ropes with gusto treating their neighbors to the peal. In some towns a standard prank was to take rocks and stones and place them across the main street to create a speed bump. Pranksters threw eggs at cars. Some youngsters borrowed a cow for the evening. Sneaking into a barn, they roped the animal, walked it into town, and left it tied to a store door. The next morning when the store owner found it, he had to check with the local farmers to find out whose cow was missing. Neither the farmer nor the shopkeeper were very happy.

Most homes in town displayed hand carved pumpkins. Moms made the costumes worn by the kids. Masks, if worn at all, were just a half cover over the eyes. Halloween was a festive time and the  town's one police officer was always relieved if the evening passed with minimum damage. The next day was cleanup time.

The Christmas pageant at the local church was an event that everyone tried to attend. Santa made an appearance and passed out his classic Christmas treats of fresh oranges and candy.

On Easter Sunday mothers and daughters showed off a new hat, dress, shoes, and a pair of gloves. Young boys also dressed up and the family went off to church. Some women wore a small cluster of fresh flowers on their Easter coat that created a very pleasant aroma. After a special service, the families returned home to a festive dinner.

Although it may seem strange to us today, another major social activity was going to the post office to pick up the mail. Mail came in three times a day but it was the 5:00 p.m. delivery that brought the folks to the post office. While the mail was being sorted, people stood around and talked about the day's activities and caught up on the local gossip. By 6:00 p.m. the mail was sorted and the postmaster called out, "That's all folks! See you tomorrow."

Post Office

After a winter snowstorm, town authorities closed one or two hilly roads to traffic so kids could go sledding. These roads were not sanded and they were blocked off by sawhorses. The children hauled sleds and toboggans up the hill and enjoyed the quick thrilling ride down. However, it was a long haul back up for the second ride. Skiers had the same experience. It was fun skiing down the steep hills, but it was a long hard walk back up, carrying skis through deep, heavy snow.

Kids shoveled off the local pond for a leisurely skate or a good hockey game. They lit a bonfire on the edge of the pond to keep skaters warm. A log near the fire, or a sled brought from home, were used as seats while putting on skates. Skates were hand-me-downs. Boys might use sister's skates or girls use brother's -- whatever fit. They were either single or double runners and some were strapped onto boots.. Until some kids really learned to stand up on their skates, it looked as if they were skating on the sides of their feet. Heavy stockings were always worn to keep the skaters' feet warm. Pickup hockey games were played on most ponds. The goals were marked by anything; large stones, tin cans, or boxes. Hockey sticks were heavily taped with black electrical tape.

Other sports played by young boys were pickup baseball, basketball, and football. They played in vacant lots, fields, and gravel pits. Someone always had a ball. Many times the owner of the ball was the worst player, and ownership ensured a place on the team. The kids chose teams by counting fingers (odd and even) or by tossing a bat. The two best players picked sides, with the first pick going to the one who won the toss. Since few boys had baseball gloves, everything was shared. Most equipment was in bad shape. Lefties wore right-handed gloves on the wrong hand, baseballs were reinforced with black tape, and broken bats were screwed back together and repaired over and over again. The competition was keen and the game was played with a great deal of enthusiasm. The players played to win. Many times the neighborhood formed a team and games were organized against teams from across town. There were no umpires so close plays were decided by an unwritten honor system.

Football games were played on grass plots with no pads or uniforms. The bladder usually showed through the ends of the ball. Once again, electrical tape was put to good use. Basketball was another popular sport. The young players hung up a peach basket on the side of an old building or barn and used it as a hoop.. Someone produced a battered basketball and the game was underway. They played with just the one basket: when a team scored or lost the ball, the other team took over the offense at mid-court. The children never expected much. They were accustomed to making do with what they had and were easily satisfied.

When the family was at home they played many board games. Checkers, Parcheesi, dominos, and card games provided hours of fun for the family. They played card games: fish, harts, solitaire and bridge. The radio was popular but lots of static came from those old tube filled boxes with the large dials. In the 1930's and 40's, family members gathered around the radio and enjoyed programs like *The Lone Ranger, Jack Armstrong, The Shadow, Inner Sanctum, The Thin Man, Fibber Magee and Molly, Jack Benny, Amos & Andy*, and programs that featured popular dance bands.

Church suppers were a favorite event. When a church supper was announced it was a delight for people who knew good food. Organizing and running the church suppers was a skill handed down from one generation to the next. Although men helped, the

Beech Ridge Church

women of the church did most of the work. For a pot luck supper, each woman prepared a special dish at home and brought it right from the stove to the church. By 5:30 p.m. the food had arrived. The men covered the long tables with white tablecloths and set up the silverware for the supper. People scooped up the goodies onto white porcelain plates. What a variety of treats awaited them. They served the food home style or buffet style. The renowned cooks in the church were well known for some delicious dishes and their food disappeared first. It was not uncommon to fetch a piece of popular pie and take it with dinner, before it disappeared. The young folks of the church served coffee, tea, and milk.

After everyone finished eating, the men washed the dishes, removed the long tables, and restored the hall to its original setting. Entertainment followed. A local church member presented a magic show, someone sang a couple of solos, or a local youngster played an instrument. If a young aspiring musician played a violin, some of the people were glad that the program concluded.

Other types of church suppers featured turkey dinner, lobster dinner, fish chowder night, or the standard, baked beans and hot dogs. One could eat as much as he wanted –portions were piled high. Most people would agree that better food couldn't be found anywhere. These suppers were well worth the modest donation collected at the door.

In every community there was a local hangout, usually a newspaper store, where the young boys gathered in the early evening hours. Raspberry cokes, five-cent ice-cream cones and one-cent gum and candy were very popular with this crowd. The boys' talked about

George A. Marshall Store

anything and everything that was happening. This was also the spot where some younger boys learned some of the facts of life. If a parent did not talk about a subject at home, it was certainly discussed on the corner. Kids made some real good buddies and many became lifelong friends. During World War II more than one group of neighborhood chums joined the same branch of the service together.

In the late 1930's and 1940's drive-in theaters were very popular. At the age of twelve, Russell Vose worked at the local E.M. Loew's drive-in. He made sure that all the speakers were hooked up and working properly and during the movie, he walked between the cars selling candy, popcorn, hot dogs, and soda. He said the views were very interesting, and on occasion, he made a few people very angry -- especially those who weren't watching the movie.

Extended families were common as grandmothers, grandfathers, aunts and uncles all lived under one roof. Large families worked together and older kids watched younger ones. Many times a newlywed couple moved in with one of their parents for financial reasons. Between the extended families people made do. There was plenty of love, companionship, and sharing. Kids went to Sunday school and participated in church programs. Both adults and youths sang in one of the church choirs. Many kids had a paper route -- not an easy job. When Russell Vose delivered the daily newspaper he was not allowed to throw it on the porch. There were no plastic bags to protect the papers and no boxes at the edge of the street. Every paper was put in a safe place where the customer was sure to find it. Newspaper deliveries were truly door-to-door jobs.

THE DEADLY FLU

In 1918, by the month of October, over 80,000 influenza deaths had been recorded in the United States. The deadly flu was referred to as the *Spanish Flu*. People were in a state of panic.

Influenza vaccine had not yet been invented, so the disease spread unchecked.

New Englanders were hit as hard as any other part of the country. Convents were turned into hospitals as the local hospitals were flooded with patients. Doctors and nurses were getting sick along with everyone else. When the epidemic struck, the victim's throat and bronchial tubes became severely inflamed. This was followed by a high fever, diarrhea, malnutrition, neuralgia, muscular weakness, and finally, complete exhaustion. Air passages, liver, and intestines were affected. It is no wonder so many people died.

Stores, factories and work places were severely understaffed as this deadly disease spread. Some towns quarantined essential public safety workers. They asked these workers to sleep at the station house or the town hall so they would not be exposed to sick people at home. Many churches closed, canceling masses and services. Schools were shut down, theaters were not opened, and the people were told to stay home. In every family it appeared that at least one or two members were sick. Doctors tried sulfur drugs against the epidemic, but they had no effect. When the plague struck a local town it spread quickly and caused widespread grief for at least two or three weeks. Some victims were able to get rid of the infectious bug in three or four days but in other cases it took a couple of weeks. Many victims did not survive, as this dangerous infection snuffed out life after life.

THE GREAT MOLASSES EXPLOSION

On January 15, 1919, a tank of molasses exploded in Boston's North End. The cause of this explosion is still unexplained.

Molasses was used in the manufacture of alcohol. A large storage tank approximately ninety feet around and fifty feet high was filled to the brim with the gooey substance. The tank was located just off Commercial Street across the road from the fire station and in a congested area. The tank was holding about 2,200,000 gallons of molasses. It had been piped-in warm, from a tanker docked in the harbor. Eventually the liquid would be drawn off and shipped to Cambridge to be made into rum. The tank was built in 1915 and this was the first time it had been filled to capacity because Congress had been considering some type of prohibition legislation. If passed, the country would be dry and the molasses would have no value. This was a concern to many people. (A year later, on January 16, 1920, The 18th Amendment was ratified and liquor was outlawed.)

It was noontime in Boston, and most folks in the North End had stopped work for a lunch break. The weather was warm. The area was filled with horses, cars, wagons, pedestrians, and workers. Many sailors and local businessmen were in the pubs. Then it happened. A rumbling noise that sounded like an earthquake was followed by a sharp piercing noise, like the sound of a machine gun. Within seconds, an explosion happened so fast that people were caught off guard. The tank had split apart.

The machine gun noise had been the popping of the rivets that held the solid iron plates together. After the rivets pulled away from the steel, the pressure and weight of the dense cargo split the tank. The top of the tank was thrown into the air and millions of gallons of liquid began to gush out of the ruptured tank. A twelve-foot tidal wave of this sticky, gooey substance descended on the area. Houses collapsed, small buildings were picked up and carried away, and even the steel support beams that carried the elevator cars were knocked out of place. Several industrial workers who had sat down to quietly eat their lunch near the tank were immediately drowned and swept away by the surge of molasses.

In just a few minutes, the thick brown mess was roaring down Commercial Street and spreading out into the side streets. It was at least two feet high in most places. Cars, pianos, furniture, wagons, and houses were lifted up by it. People were tossed about, and many were trapped and became completely submerged. The Public Works Building was torn from its foundation and the workers inside went for an unexpected ride. This building was demolished fifty yards from its location, although most of the workers were able to scramble to safety.

The firehouse was destroyed. Two firemen on duty were injured and one was killed. People panicked. Two women looked helplessly out of the second story window of their house, as it slid along the path of the molasses. The house was destroyed and both women were injured. The people who were within one hundred yards of the tank when it burst, were killed by the flood. Twenty people died that afternoon and as many as one hundred fifty were injured.

The naval ship *Nantucket* was docked at the North Pier. The captain had been on the bridge and witnessed the disaster. He recognized the severity of the situation and sounded a general alarm. He sent his men over to the disaster area to assist the wounded. The debris of falling timber and the suction of the initial giant wave had caused many injuries. The sailors waded into the mess and did what they could to help people get to higher ground. They also tried to administer medical attention to those in need. Priests arrived to administer last rites to the ones who had suffocated.

All Boston police and fire department units were called to the scene. These men assisted the sailors in locating the survivors and the dead. Ambulances arrived and the seriously injured were taken to hospitals. By 2:00 p.m. a relief station was set up in Haymarket Square for emergency treatment. People began to line up to get first aid for all sorts of injuries: cuts; bruises; sprains; shock; eye infections; and respiratory problems.

The next day contractors brought laborers and large equipment into the area to help with the cleanup. They washed the molasses away, using hot water and a salt chemical. It slowly disappeared as hundreds of men washed and swept it into the harbor waters. The area remained sticky for a long time, and people who passed through picked up the remains on their clothes and shoes. Telephone booths had sticky dials and elevator trains had sticky seats. It is said that even now, on damp days one can still detect the sweet sickly smell of molasses in buildings that survived this fateful day. The financial loss for the tank and molasses was over $300,000, but the loss of lives and property was much higher.

RUM RUNNERS AND PROHIBITION

During the first half of the 20th century, law enforcement officers faced immense headaches trying to enforce the Volstead Act, enacted on January 16, 1920. This act prohibited the sale of wine, beer, and liquor. For the next thirteen years' constables had the awesome task of shaking down the law's offenders, called *bootleggers*. Making and supplying liquor for consumers and taverns, was carried on in various ways by many people.

Some families set up illegal private stills in their cellars and barns to produce homemade liquor. This illegal liquor was sold and distributed to friends and neighbors. The law was being defied. A bad batch of homemade brew, or *moonshine* could cause serious sickness and even death.

The locals were clever and cunning in getting illegal moonshine to taverns and stores. In one town the booze was sent out in an old horse-drawn hearse. Who would check a hearse? This worked well until the day the horses bolted and the hearse ended up smashing into a telephone pole. The contents leaked out onto the street. When the sheriff arrived, he knew the puddle of suspicious smelling liquid wasn't the undertaker's usual brand of embalming fluid and he promptly arrested the bootleggers.

The term *Rum Row* refers to a constant line of ships anchored just outside the three mile ocean limit. Rum Row extended just north of Cape Cod and into Maine waters. These ships were in international waters so they could not be inspected or boarded by the United States Coast Guard. Each ship was loaded down with case after case of prized European, Caribbean or Canadian liquor. Small, fast coastal schooners and power boats sailed out, picked up a load of booze, then smuggled it back to the shore for unloading. They arrived on the beach in time to meet the local dealers whose trucks and cars transported the liquor out of the area as fast as possible. The small ships that unloaded the cargo were known as *rum runners*.

The operation was like a game. Diversions were set up on shore to distract the police or coast guard when a drop-off was scheduled. The drops usually occurred late at night under dark, moon-less skies. A fire was started at one end of town in an old building or warehouse and the constables and firemen had to rush to the location to extinguish the fire. When the fire lit up the sky, the rum running crew made the drop. With their boat loaded down with the precious cargo, they snuck into a back cove at the opposite end of town and met the waiting cars and trucks. The drop-off was very fast and as much as $100,000 worth of liquor could be delivered and on its way to market in just a short time.

Rum runners were not always successful. If their boats ran aground, the crew tried to dispose of the cargo as fast as possible. They tried to dump the bottles in the creek or hide the cases along the shore before the authorities could get to them and make an arrest. They tried to conceal all of the evidence. At times the small boat was burned before the crew fled. If the liquor had been hidden, the local folks soon found the hiding place. They knew what was going on, and in the following days, many cases of the contraband were dug up or fished out of the water. These bottles ended up in a lot of homes. Many local men told their wives they were going clamming and returned home later, under the weather, carrying an open bottle of scotch and one or two more in their pockets. When the police captured a boat, they sometimes had to fight with the local fishermen and farmers who tried to steal the cargo right out from under their noses.

Prohibition started as a noble cause. By 1920 the consumption of liquor appeared to have taken over American society. About half of the population of the country viewed drinking as evil, repulsive, and responsible for many of society's problems. The other half of the population was more tolerant and could see both the pros and cons of drinking. When prohibition went into effect bootleggers and underground bars appeared on the scene and the crime rate rose. Half of all court cases that appeared before judges had some link to liquor. This period in history is referred to as the *long dry spell*. On July 2, 1926, The House Judiciary Committee held hearings about the increase in crime and its relation to alcohol. Officials from several state asylums reported a tenfold increase in patients suffering from alcohol related diseases. Members of Congress were receiving thousands of petitions daily asking for a recall of the Volstead Act. Prohibition ended on December 5, 1933. There was still concern about the abuse of alcohol, but the majority of people were ecstatic and they celebrated the news with good, high spirits.

THE GREAT DEPRESSION

October 29, 1929 -- the stock market crashed. This day is known as *Black Thursday*. For the next twelve years, families experienced poverty the likes of which, no one had ever seen before. Factories and mills closed and jobs were severely limited. Twenty-five percent of the workforce was unemployed. Small town banks closed, some factories were boarded up, and farmers couldn't pay bills or buy supplies to keep the farms running.

In the cities, some people became scavengers. They picked through garbage pails behind restaurants, hoping to find a morsel of food. Other families picked through dumps with the hope of finding an item that might be repaired and sold for a few pennies. Dumps were also a source for materials to build tar paper sheds for living quarters. It was a sad sight to see these ashen men trying to survive in these scanty conditions. Under another set of circumstances, these people would have been called street urchins. Instead, they were just pitiful individuals making the most out of a deplorable situation. Survival was based upon courage, thrift, and a dependence on each other. Worry, anxiety, and sadness were etched on the faces of most adults.

To get through these hard times, the church became a significant factor in community life. Praying took on added meaning as neighbors prayed for the relief of each other's suffering. Churches gave food baskets to the most needy and for the holidays they included turkeys in the packages. Flour and other provisions were distributed weekly so some of the poorest families could make bread that they later shared with neighbors. The church was also one of the main centers for recreation. Other charitable groups such as the Red Men, Grange, Odd Fellows, and The American Legion organized benefits and donated the proceeds to the needy.

People tried anything to keep busy. The library was one of the most popular spots in town because the building was heated. Folks went into a room and read books and newspapers for hours. Some families had upright pianos and they organized a good old-fashioned sing-a-long. Radios were the link to the outside world, but since electricity cost money it had to be conserved, and they were not turned on too often. Phonographs provided some entertainment, since they were large, upright wind-up boxes. The records they played were made of either metal or a stiff breakable resin and the quality was not too good. Still, they played a scratchy tune or two, that provided a few moments of melodic escape.

Since cars were unaffordable for the majority, and public transportation was expensive, people walked everywhere. They started talking to neighbors and sharing their common concerns. Life was plain and people were humbled, but they remained proud. To generate the heat for cooking, young children collected wood along the river banks or along the shore. Old newspapers were rolled into logs and burned in the stove to heat baby bottles. Houses were kept fairly cold because heat had to be conserved. Kerosene space heaters, though dangerous, were placed in the coldest rooms. If knocked over they could easily start a fire and if a youngster accidentally touched the heater he could be severely burned.

Most homes had dirt cellars that remained cool and damp but made an excellent cold storage area for vegetables grown in the garden. Gardens were a necessity for anyone who had enough room to plant one. Vegetables and fruits were canned and preserved to last through the winter. The smell from kitchens during canning season was beyond description.

Because potatoes cost fifty cents a barrel they were served at almost every meal. A variety of dishes were created with meat and potato -- stew-meat pie was a favorite. Local butchers and grocers gave away scraps of food to needy families. These scraps were important ingredients in the meat pie. Liver was cheap and nutritious and used often. People occasionally ate horse meat. When the baker gave away leftover pastry, lines formed at his back door. Sometimes a fruit-truck driver intentionally dropped a box of fruit off his tailgate, knowing that a lot of hungry kids could at least have a fresh apple or orange that day.

Any fish caught by a family member were eaten for that evening's meal. Ketchup sandwiches were served often. Bread fried in lard was another cheap meal. Sugar, if available, was sprinkled over dampened bread for a special treat. Molasses was used as an alternate sweetener. Everyone ate every morsel on their plate and nothing was ever sent back to the kitchen. No food was ever thrown away. Sometimes mothers went without food if father and the children did not have normal portions. The family always came first in mother's eyes. She was also able to make something out of nothing.

People had very little money to spend and they owned just bare necessities. Telephones were considered luxury items, laundry was washed at home and hung outside to dry, houses needed paint or repairs, and the furniture was sparse. Many families out of work could not even afford a monthly rent of ten dollars and they were forced to move in with relatives. If evicted for non-payment of rent, a whole family could move their entire possessions in a couple of wheelbarrows.

Food stamps had to be earned, and in some cases they helped a family survive. Men reported to the town hall and were given three days of work on a town project to earn the stamps. Projects such as removing trees, cutting lawns, cleaning, digging, or painting were assigned to the work crew. Unemployed men from all occupations worked side by side to receive the twenty-dollar stamp that was issued directly to a local grocery store and had to be used there for essential food items only. These stamps might supply a month's worth of groceries at a cost of seven dollars a week. They just barely met the minimum needs of a family of four.

Policemen walked their beats and knew every resident by name, and every problem each faced. Often it was necessary for a policeman to spank a young boy or give him a kick in the backside if the youngster broke the law. The policemen were sympathetic to the needs of every child and the punishment usually fit the situation. Policemen were everybody's friends and they were respected by all.

When a mortgage payment was in arrears, bank officials would appear at the house and place a red flag on the lawn. This meant the house would be sold at auction, but in many cases, the bank would hold off and wait until some token payment could be made. Nobody wanted to see folks turned out into the street.

In some resort communities during the summer months, women worked for the wealthier families, cooking, cleaning, sewing, ironing and doing other housework. A few of the men and boys might find jobs as groundskeepers. Other families picked wild berries and sold them to the local grocer or baker to earn a few pennies. When a good job became available there might be over five hundred applicants for the one position. If a family earned twenty dollars per week they were considered well off.

The students who finished high school were rare. The dropout rate was high since many young people were forced out of school because of their family's financial needs. They had to find a job and earn money to help support the family. Cooperation was the key to survival. This economic sickness was harsh and people had to work together to get through these tough times.

Two or three years after the depression started, the federal government established programs to help the people. One such program was the CCC, Civil Conservation Corps. This agency was set up to feed and shelter young men in a camp environment. The boys were sent to organized camps and were paid thirty dollars per month in addition to food and shelter. They built roads, fought forest fires, worked in conservation areas, and developed natural resources. Most boys sent the money home to help their family since living in remote areas did not afford them much opportunity to spend their cash.

The Works Progress Administration, WPA, was another federal agency that employed approximately one out of three working men and women in the area. Federal construction jobs building schools, libraries, and other projects began to appear. Other jobs were created for teachers, writers, musicians, and actors. These temporary occupations brought relief to many families, but as late as 1937, President Roosevelt said, "One third of all people are ill-housed, ill-clad, and ill-nourished."

Towns that had railroad service often experienced problems with hobos and tramps -- homeless men who traveled from place to place on trains. They "ran the rails" stealing rides by hiding in empty box cars or climbing under the floorboards between the train's wheels and tracks, traveling from town to town. They were not treated kindly by the railroad security men or the conductors. In some towns they built outlandish encampments next to the tracks. Their clothing was dirty and strange looking. If a crime was committed in town, the police first suspected the hobos and tramps whom they considered drunken vagrants. This was not a desirable group to have living near town and parents warned their children to stay away from the hobo camps.

The severity and longevity of the depression are unparalleled. Humanity was tested and challenged throughout its duration. New

Englanders never lost hope. The lessons of the thirties show us how to make the most out of life's difficult situations. Stories of individuals and families, who with their backs to the wall, never gave up, and pushed on with courage and dignity, are an inspiration to us all. These folks knew from firsthand experience that storms make skilled mariners, and that the storm they were living through would pass. In 1938 Kate Smith sang "God Bless America" and as New Englanders listened, the lyrics reinforced their belief that despite its problems, America was still the greatest country in the world. The depression lasted until the United States entered World War II.

THE HURRICANE OF 1938

New England has had a lot of real bad storms, but the hurricane of 1938 stands out as one of the most destructive. A combination of things made this storm especially severe. Because New England had experienced a very wet September, rivers and streams were overflowing their banks and many dams were strained. The storm came through on Wednesday, September 21, 1938, at about four in the afternoon, just one hour after high tide. The storm's eye cut a path up through the Connecticut Valley, causing devastation all through Rhode Island, Massachusetts, Connecticut, New Hampshire, and Vermont. Maine was spared. The winds were recorded at 170 miles per hour, and tidal waves were pounding the shore. Over 680 people died and well over 1,000 were injured that fateful night. Property damage was in the millions of dollars.

At 7:00 a.m. the storm was off Cape Hatteras, having moved six hundred miles in just twelve hours. At 2:30 p.m. it was in the New York area and at 3:50 p.m. it was over New Haven, Connecticut. It was the fastest moving storm every recorded. The next morning there were floods, bridges were out, power cables and telephone wires were down everywhere. Fallen trees were blocking the roads, thousands of houses had been torn apart. Seaside homes no longer sat on their foundations and boats were left high and dry, some as far as half a mile inland from the harbor. Large factories had top floors torn off, plate glass windows in city stores were blown in, orchards were destroyed, and maple sugar trees were felled. Millions of board feet of lumber were laid waste.

In the path of the hurricane, farms crumpled up like paper bags, church steeples toppled, chimneys fell over and cemetery stones were blown off their foundations. Streets were like rivers, and downed live wires were everywhere. There were huge sinkholes in the streets and sidewalks. Trains were derailed and cars were blown over and swept into the rivers, some with people still in them. Many victims were injured by flying glass, bricks, and wood.

A Sea Village Demolished

Many folks who lived on the coast lost all of their property. They saw their houses lifted by the tide and destroyed. Many people drowned. Sporadic fires were caused by bursting gas lines, electrical wires, furnaces, and even spontaneous combustion. Yachts smashed into each other or were thrown against piers. Most of the fishing fleets were hurled right out of their harbors. At one point a fishing boat was washed up onto the main street, and was bouncing off buildings. When the boat temporarily lodged between two of the buildings, the crew climbed out through one of the building's third floor windows. In some coastal towns the entire beach area was destroyed, leaving no houses or sand dunes. Sometimes half a house was left standing, its furniture still inside, but with pipes, wires and beams exposed as though the house had been turned inside-out. In some farm areas, cattle and sheep were walking around aimlessly and poultry was scattered about all over the countryside.

All communication had been cut off except for radio. The problems were overwhelming. Medical supplies, food, clothing and shelter were the first priorities. Those who were totally stranded spelled out the word F-O-O-D on roofs and in fields. Small planes dropped them supplies. Volunteers worked in areas of great distress and neighbors helped neighbors. Federal and state agencies joined together in helping the cities and towns in cleaning up the big mess. Private individuals, churches, and service groups all gave generously of their time and funds.

New Englanders rebuilt their homes, jetties, sea walks and roads. The great hurricane of 1938 had taken a huge toll but once again, the Yankee spirit had been put to the test and New Englanders emerged unbroken.

World War II - The Home Front
1941 - 1945

Sunday, December 7, 1941, the wind chill was reminding us that winter was fast approaching. Most New Englanders had just returned home from church and were finishing Sunday dinner when the shocking news of Pearl Harbor was aired over the radio. They were stunned and angry. An uneasy feeling settled in as they began to anticipate the future. On Monday, December 8th President Roosevelt asked congress for a Declaration of War, "a day of infamy" he remarked. War was declared. During the next three and one-half years New Englanders rolled up their sleeves and did all in their power to get the war over, bring home the troops, and ensure an American victory. This was the *home front* effort.

During the days following the declaration of war, all military recruiting offices were overflowing with young men and women enlisting. Parents were proud as a spirit of patriotism and unity prevailed everywhere. At the same time however, minds were heavy with worry. The thoughts of their children being shot at far from home, and the fears of never seeing their sons and daughters again, caused many tearful departures.

The New England draft boards were busy sending out the famous "Greetings" letter notifying all men between the ages of 18 and 35 that they were eligible to be called into the service of their country. The Draft Board was composed of local men, and they alone determined the availability of local boys to serve in the armed forces. In the small towns, one board was often responsible for an entire county. Boards could give exemptions for hardship, occupations, or religious (conscientious objector) reasons. Letters signed by a member of the local board were sent out to notify draftees of their selection for training, and the draftees were given information on when and where to report. The order in which men were selected was eligible single men first, then married men without children, followed by married men with one child. The board also had the power to draft men up to age 65 if labor was needed for defense work, however, this was never necessary.

All draftees were instructed to meet at the town hall, the draft board office, or some other public building where they boarded a bus or a train and headed for training camps. The local women gave each man a "buddy pack" that contained razors, candy bars, and stationery. The departure was sad as young boys said good-by to their fiancees, mothers kissed sons, and brothers and sisters embraced. One of the saddest scenes was the expression on a father's face if the father had been a veteran of World War I. Many dads had seen war and death firsthand, and wished they could spare their children that agony. A resigned despondency, a look of hopelessness, framed their faces. It was easy to spot these veterans as they held back tears.

*Harlan Webster and son Spencer
3 Webster brothers served in WW II,
Spencer, Kenneth and James.
Spencer lost his life in Perthes,
France on September 10, 1944.*

When family members left for the war, an emptiness and a sense of loss prevailed over the town. Mothers hung small flags in the front windows of their homes that consisted of a blue star on a field of white. Some flags carried two or three stars, each star representing a family member serving his country. As the war ground on, many blue stars were replaced by gold ones, indicating family members who had given up their lives for their country. The pain and grief grew immense as more and more gold stars appeared. Women who lost loved ones were referred to as *Gold Star Mothers*. Neighbors cringed when two uniformed men or a clergyman knocked on a serviceman's door. These visits or the delivery of a telegram always meant bad news.

Each day the local paper listed the updated casualties in one column and the wounded in the next. Local libraries posted these lists on the bulletin boards for the general public and many folks stopped off on their way home from work each day to check them. People hoped and prayed they would not see a neighbor's son or a dear friend listed. It was heartbreaking and not uncommon for a letter written by the serviceman to arrive two or three weeks after the news of his death had been received. When a local serviceman died, the impact on the community was vast. Older people; religious leaders; school teachers; store keepers; everyone seemed to know and remember the veteran. They spoke of their fond memories of him. The townspeople would mourn each loss as if it was their own.

New England people began to become involved in the war effort on a personal nature by volunteering to work in any war related operations. Ration boards, civil defense, aircraft spotters, auxiliary firemen and policemen, United Service Organizations, and The Red Cross were a few of the organizations to which folks generously gave their time. After school hours young students went to work in stores and other non-essential war jobs as the older folks took jobs in defense plants and factories.

During the war years forty percent of the workers in the shipyard at Portland, Maine, were women. The women were filling jobs normally filled by men. *Rosie the Riveter* took over the workforce. Shipyards, factories, and defense plants were filled with women welders, technicians, and laborers. Women became the backbone of America's workforce, and they proved that they were as capable as men. For safety reasons hairstyles became shorter because women did not want to chance getting their hair caught in the machines. Slacks became the popular dress for factory jobs.

Portsmouth Naval Shipyard

Factories were operating twenty-four hours a day. Workers could work out a suitable shift, including overtime, to fit their special needs. The swing shift was a new term designating shifts other than the usual nine-to-five. Bus companies operated around the clock to transport the workforce back and forth from surrounding communities to the factory. It is estimated that over 12,000 people a day worked in the Portsmouth Naval Shipyard in Kittery, Maine. Other large New England industries, such as General Electric, used private bus contractors and trains to assist in transporting their workers to and from the jobs. Many defense factories and shipyards worked the crews for thirteen days straight, eight hours a day, and then gave them one Sunday off. Defense workers did not take vacations but vacation time was accumulated and used at war's end.

Small farmers were asked to produce more fruit, vegetables and dairy products, but they were not given any financial help and could not hire additional labor to meet these demands. Families dug-in and production went up. Sometimes the father would turn the small farm over to his wife and children while he went to work in the nearest shipyard or factory. Unfortunately, New England farm families were not a part of the national farm boom. Price controls and shortages hampered their growth and some farms collapsed. Many fishermen, the farmers of the sea, could not get enough gas to run their boats. Lobster, when available, was selling for 25 cents a pound. Many of the lobster men, like the farmers, joined swing shifts in local factories. Since the Government had frozen priority items, such as lumber, metal and wire, local tradesmen were also out of business. Electricians, plumbers and carpenters went to work in the defense plants.

A large number of men who were not of draft age joined the state guards and Civil Defense. Many towns and cities had their own unpaid volunteer group of soldiers. A group from a local town would be made up of fifty-six men who formed two platoons. This was a complete voluntary service whose function was to protect towns from fires and any other emergency that might occur. Drills were held one night per week and special training took place on the weekend.

To assist in the war effort, New England school children planted victory gardens, ran scrap metal drives, collected rubber products and milkweed floss (used in life jackets), organized paper drives, and wrote letters to lonely servicemen. Every week many children turned in portions of their savings to buy ten-cent and twenty-cent savings stamps. The stamps were put in an album, and when $18.75 was collected, a $25.00 war bond was issued to the child. The war was costing a great deal of money and this was one of the ways school children were involved in the fundraising. If a grandmother bought stamps or bonds for grandchildren, she could become a member of the Grandmothers War Bond League. Rallies and payroll deductions were other ways funds were raised to purchase bonds.

Scrap paper drives were organized to collect recyclables. It was not uncommon for kids to accumulate fifty tons of paper in one weekend -- enough to fill two freight cars and a trailer truck. Rubber drives collected old bicycle or car tires that after recycling, would end up as tires for military equipment. The war years were one of the largest scavenger drives in history since the whole country participated. Metal drives collected pots, pans, tin cans, used automobile parts, and street car tracks. Anything metal was collected for the war effort. String and aluminum were also recycled. People of all ages pitched in and no sacrifice was too great for the war effort.

On January 30, 1942, the Office of Price Administration was established by the Congress. Known as the OPA, this organization set price ceilings on consumer goods and rents. They also set up the programs to ration food and scarce items through the distribution of stamps. In May, New Englanders were setting up local boards to carry out the process. Men and women were both chosen to sit on these boards. There were four boards established and each had responsibility in one of the following areas: food, home fuel and oil, tires and gasoline, and textiles. If a local citizen had a specific problem, he or she went to the appropriate board for an answer or solution.

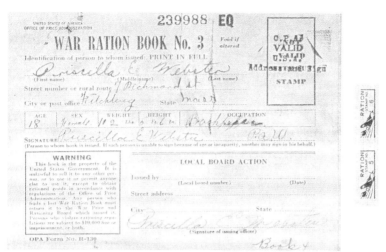

War Ration Book and Stamps

When ration books were first used local school teachers distributed the books. The coupons were given out once a month. The food items people enjoyed most were the ones first rationed: meat, cheese, sugar, butter, and coffee. They were followed later by canned fruits, vegetables and soups. Every man, woman, and child on the home front were issued these books. Each stamp had a letter and a number printed on it, in addition to pictures of PT boats and tanks that were a constant reminder of the war. Meat stamps were red and all others were blue. Rationed food was assigned points. A can of peaches might be eighteen points, and a can of carrots six. The shopper had to add up the points and make sure they had enough stamps to purchase the items. If they ran out of stamps they had to wait until the following month before they could purchase any more rationed items. The stamps represented the quantity that could be purchased. The grocer sent the redeemed stamps to his wholesaler who then credited him and replaced his stock.

Most folks lived on one pound of coffee every five weeks. Fresh pots of coffee were not brewed often as old grounds were used over and over again. People were restricted to two pounds of meat per person per week, a total of eight ounces of sugar per family per week, and one pound of butter per month (providing these items could be found). Prunes, honey, molasses, and corn syrup were used as sweeteners. Meat and fish casseroles and other new recipes extended the short supply of food. "Use it up, make it do, or do without" was the motto. Hoarding was considered unpatriotic. When the heads of households went for stamps, they were supposed to give an account of all rationed food they had on hand before more stamps were issued. Oleo replaced butter. It came in a plastic bag and was pure white. A little yellow package of vegetable die came with it and when mixed together, it made the Oleo look like butter, but it sure didn't taste like butter.

Fish made a good meal when it could be purchased. In place of meat, tripe (the stomach lining of a cow or ox), liver, and kidneys were purchased. Butchers left the bone in and the fat on when choice steaks were made ready for sale. Butchers only sold these to their best customers. It was not uncommon to find hot dogs stuffed with potatoes, crackers or soy beans. If a person ate in a restaurant and meat was on the menu, stamps were not necessary.

Women often waited for hours to buy a pair of nylon stockings. Lines would form in front of a local store and extend for two blocks as the women waited to purchase their pair of nylons. Silk, nylon, and rayon were scarce as these materials were used to manufacture parachutes. In the winter months a woman might wear woolen knee socks in place of nylons. Clothing styles changed as fabric became scarce. Padded shoulders went out, long dresses became shorter, smaller hats appeared, and slacks became fashionable. It was impossible to buy an automobile or a bicycle so family members had to share. The last automobile built for sale to the public was built in 1941 and no new cars were available until 1946. Household appliances, toasters, irons, washing machines, refrigerators and stoves were unavailable. Neighbors shared with neighbors and a true sense of community developed.

New Englanders felt the real pinch at the gas pumps. When the gas rationing program was started in early 1942, coupon books were issued to automobile owners. Each car owner was issued a large stamp to be affixed to the front windshield of the car. The stamp was printed with a large letter A-B- or -C, visible for all to see. The letters on the windshield had to correspond with the stamps in the coupon book that was used to purchase the gas. An "A" book allowed three gallons of gas to be purchased each week and "B" and "C" books permitted more. These higher quantities were given to defense workers, nurses and people whose transportation needs related directly to the war effort. Trucks, buses, taxicab, ambulances, and government vehicles always had enough gas as did doctors who traveled from house to house to care for the sick. Neighborhoods setup carpools to get to work, to shop and to attend church.

The number of pages newspapers could print were limited due to paper shortages. This was not a problem because advertisements were few since store owners did not have much to sell.

The Civil Defense was the most visible group at home during World War II. One of their major functions was to organize and run a simulated air raid. Air raid drills were practiced to prepare for the worst. If the sirens began to wail, non stop, for more than a few minutes, people were trained to take cover. School children were rushed into the basement area or to inside corridors. Some children were instructed to sit under desks. The main idea was to get away from windows. Each child was told to sit in a tucked position with arms folded around the head for protection. Gas jets and electricity were turned off and extra water and first aid kits were stored on shelves in the immediate area. Air raid wardens were assigned to every community to make sure that all precautions were obeyed.

The most frightening time was when the drills were held at night. All lights were turned off, radios went off the air and nothing moved. Large dark shades were drawn over windows and blankets or drapes were pulled over these. Not even a pinpoint of light could show through the windows. The wardens checked the houses and if they saw any light they issued a warning. Each warden was issued a helmet a whistle and an arm band and some carried gas masks. New Englanders had to strictly adhere to a constant black out every night. Automobile headlights had to be taped or painted black halfway down the lens, and speed was limited to thirty-five miles per hour, still too fast for night driving under these circumstances. Illuminated outdoor store and office signs were shut off. Street lights were also turned off and even skylights were painted black so they would not reflect moonlight. If a store was open at night owners were allowed to keep the door and window shades up to eye level only. Parking lots, amusement centers, and public ways were shut down. Outside lighting was restricted to a 15 watt bulb.

Aircraft spotters were on the job day and night. A great number of women volunteered for the day shift and men took over at night. Schoolchildren were taught to spot various types of planes, U.S. and foreign. Children who had a deep interest in planes were used as volunteer spotters after school and on weekends. Spotters worked out of a small shanty that had been built on a hill or some strategic building within the town. Each worker was issued a pair of binoculars. Every plane seen or heard was identified and recorded. If the plane could not be identified, the nearest Civil Defense office was called.

The Coast Guard and the Coast Guard Auxiliary continuously patrolled coastal shorelines. Men armed with rifles and sometimes accompanied by trained dogs marched back and forth along the rocky shores. They passed each other at regular intervals. The concern was that German U-boats would drop off saboteurs

U.S. Submarine - SS48 WWI

who would attack defense plants or attempt to poison reservoirs. Patrol boats were sent out to investigate unexplained lights or strange diesel engine sounds that occurred off the immediate shore, sure signs of a Nazi sub surfacing to re-charge its batteries. Many of these subs were chased back out to sea by the Coast Guard. Some were trapped and sunk before they could reach open waters.

Almost every New England household had a victory garden during the war years. Folks planted all kinds of vegetables to feed the family. If a home did not have enough land, the family could use town land or land donated by local farmers. More food grown meant less food to buy, which made more food available for the military. Reminders of the war were all around and couldn't be avoided. When working in the gardens or going down into town, it was common to see a large formation of new Flying Fortess bombers or P-47 Thunderbolt fighters on their way to Newfoundland where they would re-fuel and then fly off to England.

Edna Mauriello was a college student during the war years. The following are quotations from her memories of her experiences on the home front:

"The war in Europe hung heavily over us. There was always the uncertainty of where our country was headed. All the men who had started with our class in 1941 were taken into the service and gradually every man from the college had volunteered or had been drafted into the armed forces. We missed them, worried about them and prayed for them. Because of our youth we were still fun loving and enthusiastic but as the war in Europe escalated we worried about our friends and family members who were in the service. We tried to find ways that we could take part in the war effort. Besides buying War Bonds and working part time in the hospitals as nurses aids we spent the semester break in the summer months working at one of the General Electric plants in Lynn, Massachusetts. It made us feel good that we were directly involved in helping out our country. I was in a plant that was making parts for B-52 bombers. I used to go to the movies to see the bombers in the newsreels before the main feature came on. I felt proud to think that I probably helped to make these bombers fly. All of us shared snapshots of our family members and boyfriends who were in the armed forces. Very early in the war the whole college was saddened to learn of the death of our first classmate who was killed in the line of duty. He was a brilliant student and an outstanding leader. There were so many tragic deaths to follow."

"Commencement was usually a very happy and less serious day. However, for my class, commencement was a very somber day, June 6, 1944, D-Day. What should have been a very joyous occasion was marred by anxiety and worry about our fellow students who were in the service. All of us felt we shouldn't be celebrating when our country was at war. Saying good-by to our classmates was very difficult because we worried about what would happen in our lives as a result of the war and we knew that the war would change our lives."

WAR & NAVY
DEPARTMENTS
V-MAIL SERVICE

OFFICIAL BUSINESS

On June 6, 1944, the invasion of Normandy took place. New Englanders knew what had happened because every church bell in every town was rung between 9:00 and 11:00 a.m. On April 12, 1945, President Roosevelt died and Vice President Truman took over the country and the war. Radio programs were suspended for three days. Many New Englanders openly cried over the death of their beloved President. On VE-Day (Victory in Europe), May 7, 1945, church services were held and people prayed. The German armies had surrendered and the European war was over. There was no dancing in the streets because America was still at war with Japan. Many boys were in the midst of the Pacific struggle and casualty rates continued to increase. After two atomic bombs leveled Hiroshima and Nagasaki, Japan, the Japanese surrendered on September 2, 1945. VJ-Day was a day to celebrate. Everyone rejoiced and gave thanks. Most of the fighting men and women would be coming home to start a new life. Certainly there had been much sacrifice -- marriages were postponed, birth rates were down, and children did not get to know their fathers for two or three years. The greatest price was paid in the lost lives of loved ones who died in the service of their country. Yes, the sacrifices were great, but the effort of those on the home front helped ensure nothing less than complete victory.

WORLD WAR II -- THE FRONT LINES

*Sunday, December 7, 1941, "A day of Infamy"...*this day will never be forgotten. This day changed the lives of every American in one form or another. The Japanese had bombed Pearl Harbor, our airfields were destroyed, our Navy had been severely crippled and hundreds of military personnel had been killed or wounded. This shocking, brutal and evil criminal attack would catapult the United States into World War II. The next day, December 8, 1941, war was declared not only against Japan but also with Germany and Italy. For the next three and one half years every eligible young man who turned eighteen would be joining the military. Before the war would end, married men

Edward E. Clough

thirty-five and under with families, were also called upon to serve in this war.

What was it like for thousands of men to enter into the military forces and be thrust into a war? Edward E. Clough was such a person. His memories capture the abrupt turnaround in his life and the dramatic change that took place. On June 12, 1942, six months after the bombing of Pearl Harbor, Ed Clough joined the United States Marine Corps. For the next three and one-half years he would serve his country with pride, honor and integrity. He would be discharged a Second Lieutenant on November 10, 1945. I have chosen Ed's story because he represents what these patriotic American men had to sacrifice and endure to keep our country free and our great American principles intact. The following excerpts, in Ed's own words, written in chronological sequence, are a precise account of his life in the United States Marine Corps during this traumatic period of history.

The Life & Experiences of Edward E. Clough as a United States Marine

June 12, 1942, dawned bright and sunny as a group of young fellows left Worcester, Mass. in a U.S. Marine station wagon headed for the Marine Recruiting Center in Boston. Upon arrival we were conducted into the recruiting office for introductory remarks including, "The U.S. Marine Corps will make men of you."

A slight problem arose as I was taking my physical. Minimum requirements to be a Marine were 120 pounds in weight and 5 feet 4 inches in height. As of that moment I weighed in at only 119 pounds and 5 feet 3 and 3/4 inches, both below the required minimum. The Recruiting Sergeant suggested I go out and fill my stomach with bananas, popcorn and water and also ruffle my hair slightly and maybe I would reach the minimum needed. This I did and weighed in at 120 1/2 pounds and 5 feet 4 inches. We were then told to be back at 1300 (1 p.m.) hours to be sworn in.

An amusing situation developed. In our group from Worcester was a big husky farmer from Oxford, Mass. When we returned to be sworn in he never showed up. One of the other fellows stated the farm boy changed his mind and went home. After a rather impressive swearing in ceremony and another speech by a Marine officer we were marched to one of the hotels in Scollay Square and told to assemble at 8 a.m. in the hotel lobby at which time we would be taken to the train station.

Back in 1942 the trains for the most part going South were the kind you could flip and change your seat direction. They were not the kind you could lie back in. We were told we would be on the train for about 30 hours. At Washington's Union Station we had to change trains and this one was just as uncomfortable. To get a little sleep we put our suitcases in the space between the seats and this made a makeshift bed, if you want to call it such. Also, there were no air conditioned cars.

We finally arrived in Beaufort, South Carolina at 1400 hours (2 p.m.) Sunday afternoon and were transported in so called "cattle cars" across the bridge to Parris Island at Marine Corps Boot Camp, a tired, hungry and dusty group of recruits.

Our first day at "Boot Camp" was more of an indoctrination day. We were awakened at 5 a.m., shown how to properly make up our bunks (blanket tight enough so a quarter bounces on it) and off to chow at 6 a.m. Daily shaves were required whether needed or not. I had my quickest haircut ever as in about two minutes I had no hair left. In a way it was comical because you had a difficult time recognizing some of the other fellows without their hairdos. After haircuts we had our dental exams and then off to sick bay for our first series of shots (and subsequent sore arms and shoulders). Also because of the shots we were subjected to a quarantine period of one week. All we could do were close order drill, go to meals, and be confined for the rest of the time to our barracks. No one was allowed to sit or lay on their bunks until after 1630 hours (4:30 p.m.) No chairs were available so we either sat on our locker boxes or on the floor.

We were fortunate to be billeted in a red brick barracks building instead of in tents like the platoon ahead of us was given. We have two DI's (Drill Instructors) who are very strict but who also seem to be fair. They will take us all the way through our eight weeks training program. During our quarantine period they lectured us on several different subjects as well as telling us in no uncertain terms what they expect of us and the consequences of not living up to their expectations.

We finally received our 30 caliber Springfield .03 rifle equipped with bayonet and scabbard. They weigh 9.6 pounds and supposedly are the best rifle in the world for distance accuracy. The rifle had 45-50 parts which we have to learn, by name and how to disassemble and assemble within a set time. We also received our field equipment and learned how to correctly pack it.

From now on our training became much tougher. We drill every day for eight hours and by the end of our drill period the rifle feels like it weighs 50 pounds. Under the manual of arms drill we have to slap real hard after every position where our hands touch the rifle. Needless to say by the time this drill ended our hands were red and sore and in some cases blistered.

On Sunday (end of our first week) our whole platoon had to attend a short church service held by a Methodist minister. (Still in quarantine). We had our first good meal of fried chicken, mashed potatoes, gravy, peas, green beans, lemonade and ice cream. The food was, as a whole, very good and plentiful.

During our second week we had the first of several inspections by a Major. We had to dress in our khaki uniforms, complete with leggings. We surprised our two DI's as those of us who were asked questions answered them all correctly and no one had a dirty rifle. They previously had processed ten other platoons and for the first time a platoon had passed an inspection without any demerits. We were rewarded by being able to go swimming in a pool and a chance to play a ball game.

We spent part of the last three days of our second week learning various battle formations like we will use in actual combat situations. This included running in a zigzag fashion a few yards at a time then hitting the deck (ground) at top speed in mud, sand or dirty clay and also in pebbles left over from a bad nighttime thunderstorm. All this in addition to our manual of arms and marching drilling.

Our first discipline punishment prevented our platoon from viewing a graduation parade. One of the dumb southern squad leaders left his locker box out in the aisle and when one of our DI's came through to put the lights on after a practice air raid drill he stumbled over it so he put the whole platoon on report. So instead of seeing the parade we spent the time drilling with rifles and full packs. Needless to say we weren't very happy with our fellow southerner.

We started our third week off with our second full inspection. This time by the senior Gunnery Sergeant of the 3rd battalion which we are a part of. He really scares you when he looks at you or asks a question. He never smiles but the DI's say he is a real "gung ho" Marine and someone you don't want to get on the wrong side of. The overall inspection wasn't too bad but several fellows gave the wrong answers to the questions asked.

There are seven battalions on the island and the 3rd Battalion of which our platoon is in is reputedly the best Battalion of the seven so we have a reputation to maintain.

We are continuing our simulated battle formation practices and on one of the days we had to crawl 200 feet on our stomachs holding the rifles across our arms while traversing over boards, stones, and dirt preparing for the taking of a town by surprise. We were a sorry looking crew when the exercise was concluded. The dirt mixed with sweat was sticking to us and our stomachs, knees and elbows were red and scraped. I certainly slept good that night. The exercise was to train us for later on when we have to hike down to the "boondocks" when we will be exposed to sand crabs, cliffs, hilly country and swamps.

On Sunday I was able to go to church and communion. In the afternoon we went swimming after two hours of rifle drill. That evening we saw our first movie starring Ginger Rogers in "Roxie Hart". I found it only fair but it helped to pass the time. The next morning we had another typhoid injection --this time 14cc instead of

7. We will get one more next week and that one will be 21cc. After each one our arms get sorer and sorer but I will manage okay.

The weather gets hotter and hotter staying in the 100+ temperature daily and our drilling and manual of arms continue for longer periods. In preparation for our Company parade we had to iron our khaki uniforms. I better learn how to get the trouser and shirt creases in the correct specified locations.

Disciplinary problems are becoming more prevalent. Talking in ranks before meals is punishable by scrubbing "the head" (toilet area) with only a toothbrush, if you are stupid enough to have a button left unbuttoned the buttons are torn off and you have to sew them back on; if you accidentally or otherwise drop your rifle for your first offense you sleep that night with it tied to your leg; your second and subsequent drop means your rifle sleeps in your bunk and you sleep on the hard floor. Other minor lapses get you extra drill or other types of physical exercise. Some of these punishments may seem ridiculous but they are supposed to instill pride and responsibility and to keep your mind focused on what you are doing.

Yesterday's inspection was our first bad one. Some fellows were late "falling out" (lining up in ranks) and others had dirty rifles. Consequently half of the platoon (including myself) re-cleaned the squad room while the other half helped clean up the mess hall. This ran from 1800 to 2130 hours (6-9:30 p.m.) so it was a real long day without much rest. I can't complain because I have only heard 2200 hours (10 p.m.) taps twice. Usually I am asleep by then.

Yesterday was the Fourth of July but it was just another very hot day for us. They only drilled us to 1500 hours (3 p.m.) because half of the platoon ended up in sick bay with sun sickness, heat exhaustion and headaches. I drew guard duty from 2200 hours (10 p.m.) to 0100 a.m. so it was a short night of sleeping for me. Another inspection beginning our fourth week. This one was fairly short because of the heat and we were dressed in our green winter uniforms. We were real glad to shed them as the material is all woolen and a lot heavier than the khaki.

I am glad I had kept in fairly good physical condition as I have felt great and have already gained five pounds. I'm up to 125 which still leaves me the smallest and lightest in the whole platoon. We leave for the Rifle Range this week and I am really looking forward to that.

We received three new Marines into our platoon. They came from the "brig" (jail) and they really fouled up our weekly inspection. One didn't know one of the eleven General Orders he was asked (which we have to know by heart) so he had to write each of the eleven twenty times by the next morning; the second one had a dirty rifle and was sent to see the Platoon Commander. He may end up back in the brig. The third and by far the worst was asked a question by the inspecting officer and the answer he gave is not repeatable. He definitely is headed back to the brig. After the inspection and during our dismissal command of "order arms" one of our regular members dropped his rifle for the second time. That meant sleeping on the squadron floor and his rifle sleeping in his bunk. I had a couple of hours off to take a test in German with

possibility of going to an interpreter school. I'm not sure how well I did but good or bad it doesn't go against my record.

We are finally leaving for the Rifle Range which means half our "boot camp" training is behind us. Like most of our platoon very few of us have ever used a rifle (never refer to it as a gun) so it will be a learning experience. We've been told the range instructors would rather have novices because they don't have to correct any bad habits. My goals are to qualify both with the rifle and the pistol. We have eighteen days of training so by the end, hopefully, I will qualify.

Reveille at the Rifle Range is at 4:30 a.m. Early the first day we received our padded shooting jackets. Other than our usual time spent on physical drill under arms (with rifles and bayonets) we have four days of "snapping in". We learn how to adjust our rifle slings to fit the three firing positions which are standing, sitting and prone. Then we learn how to sight, aim and squeeze the trigger without using any ammunition. All this is called "snapping in". We have to do this over and over for hours at a time with time out only for our noon time lunch. It was very tiring and monotonous but exceedingly necessary.

Our platoon was lucky as we are billeted in one of the few wooden barracks. Most of the other platoons ended up in pyramidal tents or the tin huts. We also missed getting eaten alive by the swarm of mosquitoes. The food at the range is lousy plus it is served on tin plates and the different types of food end up all mixed together. The cereal and coffee are plentiful and tasty. I drink the coffee even though I'm not that fond of it. By adding enough milk and sugar it's okay. We also received our final and strongest typhoid shot but my arm wasn't too sore this time.

Our last full day of "snapping in" exercises was reduced to the morning hours only. Forty-two of our platoon of fifty-four men came down with a mild case of ptomaine poison and had to remain in their quarters. They blamed it on the beans that were served the previous supper. I had only eaten a few fork fills and suffered only a few stomach cramps and a little diarrhea.

With the "snapping in" phase of our training behind us the rest of the training will be much more interesting. These last four days were tougher than any drilling we have had and much more tiresome. We now move into the most interesting phase of our training. This includes practice firing with 22 caliber rifles; firing and qualifying with both the .45 caliber pistol and our 30 caliber 03 rifles.

I'm really excited about what lies ahead of us during the next three weeks.

Our first day of firing was anything but a pleasant one. The morning was spent with lectures on safety procedures, what we do when we are down in the "pits" where the targets are and how to use the colored markers. The use of black and white markers indicate where on the target the bullet hit. A red flag waved across the target indicates a complete miss. During lunch the clouds rolled in and it started pouring. We were told to fall out (assemble) with cartridge belts, shooting jackets, rifles and ponchos (tent like raincoats). It's very difficult to get into firing positions with a poncho on as well as to sight in on a target 200-500 yards away in a pouring rain. We found out that nothing disrupts the rifle range training schedule. We were a sorry looking bunch of Marines by the end of the day.

They don't expect you to hit the bulls-eye (inch in size) firing the 22's but to concentrate to see how good a group you end up with after firing from the various shooting positions. My groups the first day were pretty bad but I did a lot better on the second and final day. We also spent part of the afternoon down on the hand grenade course learning how to release and throw the one pound dummy grenade. Safety procedures were particularly stressed. We also saw short films on sex hygiene, first aid and ways of protecting yourself in combat areas.

We had a demonstration on how to make the new type of Russian anti-tank bomb. It's called a "Molotov Cocktail". When thrown it explodes on contact, generates a terrific amount of heat and supposedly is very effective.

The days are passing quite quickly and getting closer to our preliminary and qualifying days. In addition to our regular scheduled rifle practices we have various types of work details like straightening out the supplies in the quartermaster building. We also fill and move wheel barrows of dirt to various locations. We have had a chance to play a couple of ball games which were a pleasant diversion.

The temperature the prior three days was between 123-125 degrees and today it reached 132. It may be hard to imagine working out under the blazing sun and this heat but we do it most every day. Several fellows have come down with various degrees of heat exhaustion but so far I have withstood it fairly well.

Today was our day to work down in the "butts" which is where the targets are kept. There are target areas at 200, 300 and 500 yards. We drew the 500 yard area and the NCO in charge really keeps you busy. You're assigned a certain target and after every shot you pull down the target and raise a certain colored disk indicating the location of the bullet and the zone. If the target is missed completely (which happens quite frequently at this range) we wave a pole with a red flag attached known as "maggies drawers".

As we prepared to head back to camp (about a mile away) we got caught in a wind, rain and sand storm all mixed together. It was difficult to see more than 25 feet in front of us. We really got thoroughly soaked and our rifles and packs had to be cleaned and ready to be inspected before we could go to supper.

Our last two days before qualifying were extremely busy. Each day at 0630 a.m. we headed down to the A range and pulled and marked targets for some platoon shooting their preliminaries. We got back in time for late chow and immediately after dinner fell back out to go to the D range and fired our own rifles. After our relays finished shooting we relieved the relays in the "butts" and pulled targets while they fired. By the time we got back to camp and cleaned our rifles it was supper time. After supper we changed to our khaki uniforms and left for the movies. I came back from there and went to bed. The next day was spent similarly except the other platoon fired for qualification.

Qualifying day I made marksman barely missing sharpshooter by one point which was a disappointment to me.

Our last Saturday at the Range was a fairly easy one. We had a chance to wash our dirty clothes and signed the payroll register. In the afternoon we saw film on identifying the different types of combat aircraft being used by the USA, Japan, Allies and German. Then we spent some time learning the art of self defense against knife and bayonet charges.

Today was also payday so for my monthly pay I received $39.00 (base pay of $50.00 less two month's insurance). The first month in the Marines we received $21.00 and $50.00 per month thereafter.

We were told our platoon had a rifle qualification score of 75.8% which was the highest percentage turned in by any of the 3rd Battalion platoons for quite some time. Our DI's were very pleased with the results. Now we concentrate on the bayonet phase of our training. This is where we practice protecting ourselves from enemy bayonets by using straw dummies for stabbing purposes. In our training we leave the bayonet scabbards on and joust with other platoon members in practice. No one gets seriously hurt but it has to be practiced realistically for ones own good if and when we meet the enemy.

This final week has really been hectic as we anxiously await our graduation parade and new base assignments. We have received our "dog tags". These are two small metal discs which contain our full name, blood type, service serial number, last tetanus injection date, religion and either USMC (regular enlistment) or USMCR (the R standing for Reserve). These "dog tags" remain around our neck at all times.

By having the blood type on the "dog tags" it has saved many lives when quick blood transfusions are needed. Also once you are in combat they check your name for pay call instead of signing any payroll register. You can see how indispensable they are and so very important in identifying oneself. If a Marine is killed one tag remains with the body and the other goes to Graves Registration for recording purposes.

Our final few days were spent drilling, requisitioning new uniforms, washing our field equipment and making sure our rifles were clean. We will turn our weapons in after the graduation parade.

On August 7, 1942, I graduated with my platoon, #439, and embarked for my new assignment to Radio School, Quantico, VA. We are now Marines and no longer "boots".

When I begin our schooling, classes will run from 0740-1210; 1340-1710 and a compulsory study period from 1840-2000 Monday through Friday. We were told we would be doing in twelve weeks what usually is completed in a twenty-six week period. The graduation ratio is only 70% of those who start which means I have a lot of concentrated work ahead of me. I can only give it my best effort.

At the end of eight weeks we have to be able to receive in code at least 20 words (100 letters) per minute. This is all by Morse Code which includes the 26 letters of the alphabet and 0 to 9 in numbers. They each have their own series of dots and dashes which sounds are relayed to our earphones by a signal key. My typing ability will certainly come in handy. The last four weeks will be spent out in the field learning how to use the portable field radio sets. We will be out in the field all day rain or shine training under combat conditions. This includes combat rations for our meals.

In addition to our schooling we have fifteen minutes of real strenuous exercises first thing every morning also rain or shine. We also have close order drill three times a week. Some different from Parris Island. The weather is much nicer, better food, hot showers, free movies, gymnasium, other recreation areas and a large Post Exchange within walking distance.

Summarizing our schedule we are expected to be able to receive in Morse code four words a minute, working up to a minimum of twenty in order to graduate. We also have to be able to transmit at least sixteen words per minute. As we progress we are tested at the end of each of the four weeks. We also have courses of study in electricity, electrical theory, radio components, call signs and semaphore. Each of the academic subjects will finish with a final exam. The results of these along with our code will determine our final grade. My goal is to finish in the top ten percent of our class of one hundred twelve.

This Monday we have the biggest and most important inspection of the year. A team of inspecting officers from Marine Corps Headquarters will conduct the inspection. Saturday afternoon we started cleaning windows, washing walls and waxing the floors finishing about 2130 (9:30 p.m.). On Sunday after church we went up to DC to see Alvino Ray and his orchestra along with the King Sisters. It cost us a whole 22 cents to see the show. The dreaded inspection went off much better than we expected and our Platoon Commander was well pleased. One of the inspecting officers with white gloves on rubbed them across the tops of the window casings and never even got a smudge on them.

Monday evening we drew our field equipment including mess gear, canteen, bayonet, shelter half, blanket and poncho to go with our rifles and cartridge belts.

Our first day in the field was a disaster. We began our five mile hike to reach our Communication Platoon area (C.P.) in a pouring rain. We marched with our 40 pound Field pack on the front of our body and a 42 pound. TBX Radio set on our back. In place of the radio some others carried generators which weighed about the same. The generators are run manually and supply the power to transmit over the TBX. Even with our ponchos on to protect us a little bit from the rain we were thoroughly soaked by

Ed and Buddy Rudge

the time we reached the designated area.

Most of our field work will be what we call CPX problems. We split up into groups within a certain radius of each other. Each group has to set up their radios and using their assigned code names establish radio contact with the main CP. The Telephone Platoon has to run telephone lines to each location and connect to a portable phone network. Our radio sets can reach a radius of 25 miles under the best weather and terrain conditions. As our time in the field progresses we will be setting up, breaking down and moving several times a day. It's very interesting training and simulated as though we are in an actual combat area. We have four different types of radios to learn about because before our final Marine Corps field set exam is taken we have to memorize the inside diagrams of each of the sets and the functions of each component, the front dials and other switches, range in miles of each type, frequencies and power output, types of tubes and miscellaneous other data. So I have my work cut out for me. That's the technical part of the exam, the other part is being checked out on the sending and receiving the Morse Code.

Our last week in the field was the wettest and muddiest you can imagine. It rained continuously and our trails were inches deep in mud and up to our ankles. Our dungarees and boots never had a chance to dry out and it made operations very difficult. Surprisingly very few of us came down with colds.

The continuous rain caused our whole base to be restricted and Washington DC was closed to all the armed services. Bridges from Washington to Richmond, VA had been washed out and DC was so crowded that hotel reservations were non-existent. Our power supply has been so low we have been two nights with no lights in our barracks.

We take our final Marine Corps Field Set exams on Thursday and graduation will be on Saturday, the 24th of October 1942. With a little bit of luck on my finals I should graduate very close to the top of my class and receive my Private First Class stripe. Believe it or not I now weigh 144 pounds (fully dressed) and have reached 5 feet 6 inches.

Our week furlough starts right after graduation before I have to report to Camp Lejeune on November 1st. I sure will be glad for the few days at home with a chance to see my family once again (including home cooked meals and bake goods).

I have arrived at Camp Lejeune, NC Fleet Marine Force and have been assigned to Headquarters Co., 3rd Battalion, 21 Marines, 3rd Marine Division. I will be in the Radio section of the Battalion Communication Platoon. We also have a Wire Section and a Message Center. To my great surprise my best friend, Buddy Rudge from Worcester, MA, is in the tent right beside mine. He is in the wire section.

So far our training has consisted of running different types of obstacle courses and working out in the "boon docks" (woods) with our radio sets. We also have had lectures on Chemical Warfare, Enemy Aircraft identification and miscellaneous other subjects. We will also be instructed on how to use our gas masks as well as a practice trip through an actual gas chamber. We will have to just open the side of the mask which lets in a little of the tear gas. Our eyes ran and smarted once we did that. We turned in our 1903 rifles for the new Reising Sub Machine gun. It's much smaller and lighter in size and weight and has a cartridge clip of 20 rounds. It can be fired singularly, semi-automatic or fully automatic. It's only accurate at close range. We are learning the nomenclature of the weapon and how to assemble and disassemble for cleaning purposes. We will get an opportunity to practice firing it before we leave here. We will have more practice using the semaphore flags and will have to be as efficient with them as we are with our radio codes. These are various types of signal flags each one meaning a different word and are very useful for signaling from hilltop to hilltop if the radio contact, for some reason, can't be made.

Today, November 10, 1942, is the 167th anniversary of the founding of the U.S. Marine Corps. They have cake cutting ceremonies at the Officer's Club but we as enlisted do no celebrating which is okay with me.

Even though we are down in North Carolina the weather has been real cold, going down below freezing the last few nights. We have no heat in our eight man tents so we get dressed in a hurry once reveille sounds. We usually fall out for breakfast in our overcoats and with gloves.

With most of our communication equipment already packed and ready for the staging area my days have been spent playing ball, reading books, writing letters or laying on my bunk listening to the radio. Some of the fellows spend their time playing cards of one type of game or another.

They decided to run us through one more obstacle course and unfortunately I ended up with a minor accident. We were climbing one of the vertical apparatuses when the fellow above me happened to slip. When I attempted to grab him the slippery rope plus his weight caused us both to fall into the barbed wire entanglement beneath us. To protect my face I put my hands down and my right one got cut and scratched. Our Navy Corpsman bandaged it up – nothing serious but it will be sore for a few days. It could have been worse as I ended up with his full weight on top of me.

Our last day here was rather hectic. Right after morning chow we had a talk about our conduct on the train and what equipment we would take with us. At 10 a.m. we fell out again with our transport packs assembled and inspected by our Commanding Officer. Transport packs include personal items, socks, skivvies, change of outer garments with your shelter half and blanket rolled up to fit over your pack. After lunch we had to pack our seabags and at 1500 (3:00 p.m.) fell out again fully equipped for a Company inspection by the Battalion Colonel. We were finally dismissed at 16:30 (4:30 p.m.).

We leave tomorrow, November 20, 1942, by troop train for Camp Eliot, CA. It will take us seven or eight days to reach our new location. No one will be allowed to get off the train except when we have our morning physical drills. It appears we will spend this Thanksgiving in route.

At Camp Eliot we will be living in regular type barracks. Camp Eliot is about 16 miles south of San Diego. The first couple of days were kind of quiet. Both days we have been on 10 mile hikes and one afternoon we spent on the rifle range firing our Reising sub machine guns. We also had a school session on how to decipher code by use of secret deciphering cylinders. It's complicated but very interesting and hopefully, I will get to learn more about it.

Yesterday afternoon all military facilities on the entire West Coast were put on full alert. A report had came in indicating a squadron of unidentified ships were sighted approaching the coast. Fortunately it was a false alarm but remembering what happened at Pearl Harbor we weren't going to be caught by surprise again.

As every Marine has to pass a swimming test I took and passed mine without any trouble. The pool temperature was only 52 degrees so I didn't stay in any longer than necessary. Those who fail have to take lessons at the San Diego YMCA until they can qualify. We continually work with our TBX radios and also had more sessions on Radio Theory and Electricity Fundamentals. Another gas mask drill and gas chamber pass through caused some more tears and smarting eyes. This made us realize just how important our gas masks are. The practice time we spend on putting them on as quickly as possible could possibly save our lives sometime in the future.

We had our first night problem from 2000 (8:00 p.m.) to 0100. After hiking to a canyon about four miles away we split up into 4 groups -- each one using one of the four surrounding hills. The object of the exercise was to climb to the top of the hills as quietly as possible and then make radio contact with the other three stations on the other hills. Each group was assigned their specific identifying call signs. It was slightly difficult climbing through unknown territory with a radio set on my back. By the time we hiked back to camp we didn't get much time to sleep.

Things didn't get any easier because at 6:30 a.m. we started out with heavy marching equipment on a 30 mile hike. I thought I walked fairly fast but keeping up the pace set by our Lieutenant changed my mind. We hiked down to the Mexican border and back averaging five miles an hour with a five minute rest period each hour. It was up and down hills the whole distance. Only a few dropped out due to blisters or heat prostration. When we got back our Lt. Informed us that before our training here ends he expects us to average seven miles per hour. We thought once we got back our day was finished. However at 1515 hours (3:15 p.m.) we had to go out and run the obstacle course. I don't believe I was ever that bodily tired in my life. Thankfully we have a leisurely day on Sunday.

The first morning of the new week began our jui-jitso training which we will continue with during our stay here. Any of this type of training will increase our chance of survival if and when we meet the enemy.

Our longest hike ever covered a little more than 38 miles over a ten hour period. The pace was a little slower than our previous long one but some of these hills in our training area are really steep. One hill in particular that we climbed was just about perpendicular and almost 1000 feet high. With our 42 pound radio sets on our back plus our field pack and weapon we were pretty well loaded down. One bad feature about the land out here is that it's pretty wide open with very little shade. It's mostly covered with sage brush and the sun just beats down on you. We started out with 26 in our platoon but only 16 finished this long grueling hike.

When not on long marches we usually hike out to our CPX training area where we practice radio transmissions between assigned areas. Then back in our camp areas we practice code for two hours and finish up the day by running the obstacle course. We can see the improvement our platoon is making as our training progresses.

Our next 12 mile hike will be alternating between a fast walk mile then a mile trotting. This pace should enable us to make our goal of 7 miles per hour average. We probably won't make the average the first time but will gradually work up to it. As you can see our training gets harder as each week passes but also our physical condition coincides with the training cycle.

We are leaving camp for our first real maneuvers. We go upstate to Camp Dunlop (175 mile trip) by truck convoy and we will be bivouacking for three nights. Our field problem will be conducted under practice artillery fire and we will be a part of the 7000 Marines participating in these maneuvers. We will have our first occasion to sleep in our two man pup tents.

Our truck trip took us eight hours to reach our destination which was out in the desert area. As things turned out we didn't set up our pup tents but dug a hollow hole and laid our bed roll in it and slept under two blankets and the stars. The desert is very hot during the daytime but it gets plenty cold at night. We slept for the three nights in our clothes. We were up every morning at 0530 and moved out at daybreak. Each night we slept in a different area and for two of the nights no fires or lights were allowed because we were supposedly being watched by an unseen enemy. During the day real artillery shells were flying over our heads as we gradually advanced in an imaginary attack. A couple of times I had to ride in a jeep and they were the bumpiest rides of my life. The jeeps didn't go by roads but directly across the sandy, rocky terrain. A roll of telephone wire was attached to the back of the jeep and the wire man with me laid telephone lines to each of our different CP locations. At each location we set up our radio sets and using our call signs checked into our Battalion network. We did fairly well the tasks assigned to us and besides being very interesting the experience gained will be very helpful in the future.

Our truck ride to and from the desert was mostly through mountains and we were none too warm either way. All the mountains out here are covered with rocks and cactus and after sitting on wooden seats for eight hours we were slightly lame in certain body areas.

Our return stay at Camp Eliot was a very short one. We spent a very quiet New Years eve and were able to hear some of the Rose Bowl football game. On January 2, 1943, we boarded the U.S.S. Franklin Bell which was to be our home for most of the next three weeks as we begin three weeks of practice landing and shore maneuvers.

As expected our sleeping quarters are very crowded. We have steel bunks four high. Although I have a top one I have a little more head space and won't be subject to someone accidentally stepping on me. This sea going exercise will be a new adventure to me as well as to the majority of the rest of the fellows. The ship we are on is a big one but the ocean waves really cause it to roll. A number already have been seasick but so far except for feeling a little woozy a few times I have weathered it.

Life aboard ship is quite different. For security reasons the exterior part of the ship is completely blacked out. We can only have water certain hours of the day and never after 1800 hours (6:00 p.m.). The food is plentiful and much better than we had at camp. We have been making one or two landings a day or night and they are very interesting. We got up on Thursday morning at 0300 hours and up to noontime the following Saturday I didn't get a wink of sleep. By 0430 we had climbed down our cargo nets into the small Higgins landing craft. We rode around in them in circle zones until we hit the beachhead area just about dawn. Even though they hold half of our Communication platoon they are like tiny dots in the ocean and they really roll around with the waves. We established our CP once on land and I stood radio watch all Thursday night. On Friday we continued the exercise and I was supposed to be able to sleep that night. It didn't work out as we were called out to fight a nearby forest fire. (Probably caused by one of our artillery shells). By the time we boarded our landing craft to return to the ship it was under control. Many acres were burned and many Marines were injured by burns or falls. I was very lucky and only had a few minor burns but was all black from the smoke and soot. We got back to our bunks about 10:00 a.m. Saturday morning dead tired.

I should explain a little about the equipment we carry when we climb down the cargo nets which hang over the side of the ship. We have our steel helmets, shelter half, life belts, gas mask, Reising gun, cartridge belt with clips plus our 35-42 pound radio set. This equipment totals in excess of 70 pounds so it gets a little heavy after awhile. To climb down a cargo net you line up in rows of threes and go over the side using your right leg first. When we climb down or up you hold on to the vertical rope strands so the group following does not step on your hands. When you approach the bottom of the net you have to be very careful particularly if there are ocean swells in the area. Before you release your hold on the net to get into the landing craft be careful as for one second the boat is right at the end of the net and all of a sudden because of the swells it could be 4 to 12 feet below you. Many injuries result from this type of ocean.

In our three weeks of maneuvers we made 8 different landings. Our final one was of 5 day duration. We landed on one side of San Clemente island (which is fairly large) and our objective was to seize the airfield about 30 miles away up and down the other side of the mountain. Preceding our landing 4 naval warships assisted by approximately 50 torpedo dive bombers bombed the beachhead. As our whole 21st Regiment was involved every time we moved we had to stay in contact with the 3 Rifle Companies and the Heavy Weapons Co. of our Battalion as well as with the Regimental Command Post (CP).

We lived strictly on "C" and "B" rations. The "B" ration consisted of a can of 5 crackers, 3 sugars, small can of instant coffee, cocoa or lemon powder and 3-5 hard candies. The "C" ration had a can of either hash, vegetable stew or meat and beans. The only meal we could heat them was at noontime as no fires were allowed after sunset or before dawn. The nights were very cold but the days fairly warm. The third day aboard ship one fellow in my Radio Platoon came down with diphtheria so we were quarantined for a day. We were injected twice and after reading our arms two days later 20 of our fellows were sent to Camp Pendleton for 5 days. During their absence we made one landing in San Pedro harbor in rubber boats. The last morning we left the ship the sea was very rough with swells 10-15 feet high. No one in our boat was injured but in other boats two or three fellows had broken legs and others injured from being banged up against the side of the transport. We sure were glad to get back safely on board the ship. We definitely learned a lot from our three weeks of maneuvers and ignoring the rain and cold it was a very interesting experience. We carried out our assignments quite well and were complimented by our Battalion Commanding Officer.

We didn't return as expected to Camp Eliot but ended up in Las Pulgas Canyon which is a short distance from Camp Pendleton, the largest   Marine Base on the West Coast. The 9th Marines which are part of our 3rd Marine Division are expected to ship overseas on January 25, 1943 so hopefully we can move into their barracks. We now live in large tents with no floors and no electricity of any kind. To make conditions worse it has been raining hard and the whole camp area is a large mud bowl. As our blankets and bed rolls didn't get here the first night none of us got much sleep because of the cold and wet weather.

They trucked us into Camp Pendleton for a day and for the first time in over three weeks we had a warm shower, shave and haircut. Before we returned to the canyon we had a chance to see the live Kay Kaiser show which was terrific.

Back at camp that Wednesday evening around 1900 hours (7:00 p.m.) it began to rain but by then I was nice and warm in my bedroll. About 2300 hours (11:00 p.m.) I and my tent mates were awakened because the wind had pulled up our ground pegs on one end of the tent and it was snapping. We managed to get it secured and tried to go back to sleep. However, about 0200 hours an N.C.O. routed us out to join a working party to help reset up some officer's tent that had collapsed. One can imagine how much we enjoyed getting out of our

Buddies

warm sacks into a gale. We were soaked through in no time. From that time until Saturday night we didn't get any more sleep.

In the morning our whole tent camp was a mud pile. The only dry place was inside our tent because we had the foresight to dig a trench all around it. The pyramidal tents are fairly large and can sleep six Marines fairly comfortable. There is a set way to set them up and tie them down securely. It continued to rain hard all day Thursday and by Friday we were ankle deep in mud and actually marooned as the roads leading into the canyon were impassable even to our heavy trucks. Our tents supposedly waterproof began to wet through in spots. We were called out both nights to help others with tent problems. The wind at times was so strong it was very difficult to make any headway against it and the rain continued to come down in sheets. Finally on Friday a couple of our trucks got through and I had a chance to ride into Pendleton for supplies. On our way in we could see the ocean. The waves were about 20 feet high and the whole beach area was flooded. We later learned it was the worst storm they had seen in 20 years.

Saturday we moved into our barracks at Camp Pendleton and what a relief to get dried out, regular chow and an uninterrupted night's sleep. Sunday was spent washing and drying our wet clothes and cleaning all of our equipment. The next ten days or so will be spent mostly between physical drill periods and working parties. All of our equipment has to be painted and re-stenciled.

We now have a full blooded Navaho Indian in our Radio section. With our voice operated radios he will be sending messages in his native language to other Marine units who also have Navahos. The Japanese intelligence will not be able to decipher any message that they might intercept. To me their language is all grunts and groans. He seems to fit right in and we call him "Chief".

We had our cholera shot today and I can barely use my left arm because of the soreness. We will be getting a few more different shots and one final physical before we ship out. We played and won our last basketball game which gave us the 21st Regimental championship and a large size trophy for our 3rd Battalion.

We have just arrived back at camp after 3 ½ days out in the California foothills on our final Battalion exercise. We were put through an intensive "commando type" training session exposing us to live mortar shell, machine gun fire and rifle fire. Lectures on and actual practice dealing with camouflage, types of barbed wire entanglements and trenches of various kinds were held. One afternoon we hiked 3 miles up a mountain to a cliff approximately 150 feet high. We were taught how to lower ourselves by use of a long rope. It was pretty scary but I made it down okay. The hardest part was climbing back up hand over hand. Some fellows were scared and weren't compelled to do it and one Marine fell about 25 feet. Fortunately the dirt pile at the bottom was fairly soft so he only got a little shaken up.

The 4th Marine Raider Battalion Camp was about 3 miles from our bivouac area and they made a habit of conducting night raids on the surrounding camps. One night our Lt. decided we would go on a scouting party looking for them. After about three hours of crossing brooks, fields and woods we returned without any success. Later we heard they captured two "I" company guards and threw them in the nearby creek.

The second night out it poured and the water overflowed the trench we had dug around our "pup tent" and we ended up with wet bedrolls, blankets and clothes. Fortunately it stopped by the next morning before we went out to the demolition area. As we walked through a 175 yard designated route every few yards a live grenade or small bomb would explode nearby. We had to hit the deck (ground) to keep from being hit by flying stones and dirt. We spent the afternoon making a human bridge across a river. This was done in hip deep rushing water. As soon as each man goes into the water he locks arms with the previous one and once the bridge reaches the other side the procedure is reversed until all are back on dry land. Sometimes a good swimmer will carry a rope across and secure it on the far side. Then we use the rope to hold onto as we proceed across. Later we had to cross a ready made bridge of three ropes. We crossed a small gorge by holding onto the two side ropes and tight roping across on the third. It wasn't a very easy task because of our equipment load.

The last morning we were able to make our own breakfast of eggs, bacon, potatoes, and bread. It didn't come out too badly and in no time at all it was all gone. Although the "commando training" was very interesting we were glad to return to camp and get cleaned up once again.

I have finished all my injections and passed my physical in fine shape. I now weigh 147 pounds fully clothes. We leave Camp

Pendleton tomorrow February 12, 1943, to board a ship that will take us somewhere in the Pacific.

On February 12, 1943, I left the United States aboard a converted luxury liner the U.S.S. Lurline. Most of our 21st Regiment of over 5000 Marines were aboard it. Because of its size, speed and maneuverable capabilities we were without any kind of escort.

Life aboard ship was not very exciting. Each day we had our physical drill under arms early in the morning and again in the afternoon. All kinds of military lectures were given on subjects such as chemical warfare; types of tropical diseases peculiar to the islands we may end up at; the dangers and consequences of contacting venereal diseases, first aid; Japanese weapons and aircraft and others. Most of them were quite interesting and instructional. Most nights we were able to see first rate movies. Several times we had practice abandon ship drills where each platoon had a designated area to assemble at. We used the "buddy system" and each drill was timed to see how quickly we could reach the assembly areas. Everyone took this particular practice drill very seriously because of the potential Japanese submarine danger. We also had plenty of time to read, play cards or sleep. No letter writing was allowed.

Living quarters were very cramped with four bunks high for sleeping. I managed a second tier one that wasn't too bad. Food aboard ship for the most part was quite plentiful and good. Fresh water was available an hour in the morning and for another hour around 1800 hours (6:00 p.m.). No one was allowed to delay in the portable showers or lavatory area. Fortunately the seas were relatively calm for most of the journey. When possible my friend Bud and I would spend time up on one of the open decks. The Pacific ocean is a myriad of various combinations of blue depending what depth we were passing over. At night the florescent colored fish would present spectacular sights of colored lights as schools of them followed our ship. During the day whole schools of flying fish would take off on short flights.

On the 22nd of February 1943, we crossed the equator and we had quite an unusual experience. King Neptune and his Royal

Staff prepared to initiate thousands of so called "slimy polliwogs" into his realm of "shellbacks". From Marine private up through our commanding Marine general all were subject to various types of "torture". A few of the higher ranking officers had their hair shaved off -- others had a vile smelling shampoo poured over their heads -- one or two were coated with flour and oil. One Colonel was stripped to his underwear and made to crawl on his stomach up to Neptunus Rex and had to kiss his slime covered feet. Most of us only had to pass through a gauntlet of "shellbacks" who were armed with large paddles and other types of clubs which they liberally used

as we passed through to King Neptune where we were forced to kneel. At that point he gave us his acceptance as fully recognized "shellbacks". Upon the completion of this interesting ceremony we were given a nice certificate and ID card verifying that we had crossed the equator and welcomed into the realm of Neptunus Rex. The equator divides the northern and southern hemispheres.

The only stop we made between California and New Zealand was at Noumea, New Caledonia. This was a French owned island. We weren't allowed to leave the ship as our stop was of short duration while supplies were being loaded.

On February 26, 1943, we crossed the International Date Line which meant we lost one calendar day. This is an imaginary line between the North and South Pole running along the 180th meridian. Going east to west meant changing the calendar forward one day.

Finally after 17 days of not seeing another ship (other than our stop at Noumea) we landed at Auckland, New Zealand. We were very glad to be able to stretch our legs on terra firma once again.

Our 3rd Battalion Camp was on the outskirts of the small village called Warkworth. The area was a converted large sheep pasture. Our only close neighbors are cows, sheep and geese. The surrounding scenery looks a lot like home with the hills, valleys and farmland. We are billeted in 4 man huts with no heat. The weather here in February and March is quite cold. We put water in our steel helmet shell at night and when we go to shave in the morning it is coated with ice. However, we have blankets to keep us warm at night and have gotten used to shaving and showering in cold water.

Our training here is similar to that which we had back in the States. We have many CPX problems and long hikes out in the surrounding hills (some of which are real steep). We have been to the firing range several times to keep in practice.

Every two weeks we get one day's liberty to go into Auckland, a large city that is about 45 miles away. By jeep or truck that's about an hour away but unfortunately that isn't how we are allowed to go. On liberty days we are up at 0400 hours (4 a.m.) and ready to board our trucks at 0600 (6 a.m.) for a 12 mile ride to a small train station. It took these ancient trains three hours to get us to Auckland.

In order to get back to camp we had to make sure we boarded the train by 2300 hours (11 p.m.). About three hours later we arrived back where the trucks awaited us. Finally we would arrive back at camp about 0300 hours (3 a.m.). With reveille every morning at 0600 (6 a.m.) we weren't able to get much sleep. One interesting thing during our truck rides was seeing the many big jack rabbits running and jumping along the side of the road.

Liberty days in Auckland were a little different than in the USA. Normally the first thing we did was to go into one of the restaurants and have steak, eggs and fries for breakfast. Beef and lamb were plentiful and cheap as well as being a nice change from our chow at camp. Most of their pastries, which I ate a lot of, were baked right at the restaurant.

In April 1943, we boarded the U.S.S. President Hayes for practice landing exercises and CPX problems along an uninhabited part of the New Zealand cost line. On one of the landings I came very close to having a possible serious accident. I happened to have a TBX radio generator as my back pack, and as I went to grasp the cargo net in preparing to climb down all circulation in my arms had been cut off because of the way my straps were secured and I came very close to pitching forward over the side of the ship. Fortunately the Marine lined up right behind me was able to grab my trouser leg thus preventing my toppling over. What a weird and scary feeling but I was lucky and thankful I was saved. I made sure that it never happened again.

Our rugged intense training with both day and night exercises continued right up until we broke camp for our next destination. I left New Zealand on July 23, 1943, on board the U.S.S. George Clymer and landed on the island of Guadalcanal on July 30th. From a distance the island with its tall palm trees and white sandy beaches is really beautiful. The ocean water with its various shades of blue was very warm. The Higgins boats (small landing craft) took us to about 12 feet from the shore so we dropped over the sides with full packs and gear and waded the rest of the way. Several of my Platoon ended up in water over their heads as they unfortunately fell into one of the many holes made by either dropped bombs or naval gunfire. Once on land we quickly dispersed inland to a huge coconut grove where we set up camp.

Wire Platoon - Guadalcanal

Guadalcanal is at the southern end of the Solomon Island chain. Prior to the Japanese invasion it was a British possession. The majority of its inhabitants were natives who lived in villages scattered throughout the island. Its total area was only about 2500 square miles. A number of the natives were used as scouts and their knowledge of the island was a tremendous help in locating Japanese positions as well as alerting our troops to possible ambush areas.

By the time we landed on Guadalcanal the island for the most part was secured. However, there were still isolated pockets of Japs hiding in caves and in uninhabited areas. On one of the patrols I was on, we had three native scouts with us. They could tell how old a trail was, how many enemy soldiers were in the group, what direction they were going etc. For one meal the Native Scouts caught and roasted native pigeons for us. The meat was stringy and slightly strong in taste but better than our field rations. They also showed us which plants and berries were edible and pointed out which were poisonous. We followed one stream that came down from the mountains and crossed and re-crossed this stream about twenty different times. At each of the two native villages we came to we had to receive permission from the native chief to pass through. These chiefs lived in style as they had large U.S. or Japanese tents, bunks, all kinds of cases of food supplies. The women do most of the work including planting and tending the gardens. The men did practically nothing but lay around all day smoking pipes or U.S. cigarettes. What clothes the men wore were mostly GI issue and the women wore only drab colored skirts. Their hairdos were something else, dyed in various colors. Many wore nose rings, necklaces of shells and animal claws.

Nightly air strikes from Jap bombers were very frequent. On one occasion when I was on an unloading working party down on the beach we had a visit from several enemy planes. One of our supply ships was hit and set on fire and several Navy men were killed or wounded. Fortunately (although a little late) our fighter planes from Henderson Field (Guadalcanal airfield) drove them off. Two of the enemy planes were shot down. Around evening mealtime most every day we had a visit from "Washing Machine Charlie". This was a small Japanese observation plane who was more of a nuisance than anything else. It interrupted our meal as we had to seek safety in our trenches as we never knew what part of the island he would fly over. He seemed to lead a charmed life as he flew so low and our anti aircraft guns were not very effective in hitting him.

Most of our training was conducted in the morning as we had to get acclimated to the tropical temperature which was normally 100+ degrees and quite humid. We had to take daily salt and atabrine tablets. The latter was to lessen our chance of getting malaria. On one of our patrols into the interior I corralled a large lizard (about 2 feet in length) and brought him back to camp at the end of a rope. Being in the Radio Platoon he was named "Sparky".

I kept him as a pet for a couple of weeks and then let him go. Guadalcanal had no snakes but thousands of small lizards and chameleons. You had to constantly check your bunks and boots as they were all over the place. They were harmless but some of the spiders were poisonous.

One thing there was no shortage of was coconuts. The natives showed us how to husk them to get at the fruit. I wasn't too fond of the milk but the coconut meat was very tasty. You couldn't eat too much of it at a time as it would cause diarrhea. The natives were amazing as they would scamper up and down these 50-60 foot trees to knock down the coconuts. Other than a few banana trees I don't recall seeing any other native fruit trees.

It gets dark very early on the island but when the full moon was out it was bright enough to write my letters or read a book which I did quite frequently. Unless I had guard duty I usually went to the outdoor movie. We usually had a different picture most every evening. Our seats were large coconut tree logs. While on Guadalcanal we were in the dry season with only an occasional thunderstorm to give us rain. On several evenings the movies would be interrupted because of Jap bombers hitting various parts of the island. One raid in particular was a fairly large raid and our fighter pilots knocked four or five of them out of the sky. It was sort of a spectacular view as we could see the tracer bullets from both sides firing at each other. The Tenaru River was on the outskirts of our camp area so during free time we had a chance to go swimming in it. This river was in the forefront of several major battles before we arrived.

As October and early November arrived our training became much more intensive and rumors were flying indicating we would soon be going into combat. We didn't know where but it really didn't matter as one island was similar to another and all were heavily defended. On November 15, 1943, rumors became a fact as half of my Communications Platoon including myself went aboard the U.S.S. McKean. This ship was a World War I two stack destroyer converted to a troop carrier. Once on board we learned we were headed to engage the Japanese at Empress Augusta Bay on Bougainville, British Solomon Islands.

The ship being a converted destroyer was rather small but more maneuverable and speedier than most of the other ships in the convoy. For this reason we were part of the perimeter patrol area. On the night of November 16, I had gone topside to curl up in one of the forward gun sections. However, about 0200 hours on the 17th I woke up in a hurry because the convoy guns were firing at numerous Japanese bomber and fighter planes who were attacking us. I had moved down under the canopy at mid-ship when out of nowhere a Jap torpedo plane loosed one or two torpedoes that struck our ship halfway between mid-ship and the fantail (rear of ship). The concussion knocked me face down on the deck and as I turned over I could see one of the landing craft in flames and thought the whole ship was on fire. All hell broke loose and panic set in. Two or three of the lifeboats loaded with troops and sailors were launched from the wrong side of the ship and down into the burning oil. Others just jumped over the side also into the flames. Their screams of pain were with me for a long time. The order to "abandon ship" was given a couple of minutes after the torpedo hit as the ship was sinking fast. I jumped into the water away from the flames and got rid of my boots and most of my clothes. Between my life preserver and holding onto some floating debris I was able to stay afloat. The ship went down in less than ten minutes. About 50 Marines including some very close friends and about half of the crew lost their lives. One of my telephone lineman friends, (a big Polish fellow from PA) who could just barely swim had the wherewithal to go below to get his field transport pack from his bunk and used that to hold onto while he was afloat in the water. The worst part of the ordeal was listening to moans and cries for help from the wounded in the water. Supposedly we were in shark infested waters but apparently the burning oil on the water kept them away.

While in the water I had a first hand view of the air and sea battle that went on until almost dawn. The tracer bullets and anti-aircraft missiles really lit up the sky.

Six of the enemy planes were shot down. All I could do was float around in the water and only swam when the ocean currents carried me back near the flaming oil area.

Several times we crossed and re-crossed where the ship went down as we would be in and out of masses of floating debris.

One of the odd things to happen to me and several others was the loss of our wrist watches. The explosion from the torpedoes ripped the watches themselves off our wrists leaving only the outside casings and aluminum straps intact. Other than a slight burn where my watch was I was fortunate nothing else happened to me. I guess someone up above was watching over me.

Even though the ocean in that area of the country was fairly warm by the time I was picked up after being in the water for about five hours and having only my underpants and jacket on I began to shiver. Maybe it was a reaction from all that had happened.

Along with the other survivors on our ship were two of the Jap pilots who had been shot down. I was thoroughly disgusted when I arrived on the deck of the rescue ship as they picked up the two Jap pilots, wrapped them in blankets and took them below for interrogation. The survivors from our ship of which I was one had to stand around on the hot steel decks (mostly barefooted) for up to one half hour before blankets were handed to us and led below deck. We finally were issued new clothing including steel helmets and weapons.

When I finally landed on one of the beach landing zones of Empress Augusta Bay it took me awhile to find where my Communication Platoon was located. The beach area itself had troops, tanks, amphibious tractors, trucks and landing craft all over the place. Fortunately as I had started inland to catch up with my platoon I missed the strafing of the beach area by Japanese fighter planes. Several hundred yards up the road I saw my first dead Jap soldier. Not a pretty sight to see plus he was the first dead person I had ever seen.

At just about dusk I finally joined up with my platoon. My good friend, Buddy Rudge, from Worcester had dug a foxhole for me. It was a good thing he did as that night some Jap bombers came over our area and dropped "daisy cutter" type bombs. These are bombs that are set to explode just prior to reaching the ground showering the area with thousands of small but deadly pieces of shrapnel. Two young Lieutenants who were in our area as artillery forward observers stupidly strung rope hammocks between two trees instead of digging foxholes. When daylight came only body parts of the two were found.

I found out that the U.S.S. McKean was on its final trip before returning to Hawaii for rest and refurbishing. About 50 Marines from my Battalion and over 140 sailors lost their lives when the ship went down.

The jungle and terrain on Bougainville were said to be the worst of any island in the South Pacific. For the first 1000 yards or so the terrain was very swampy. The jungle was so thick we didn't dare use our mortars or grenades. At times we could hear the Japs talking but couldn't see them. Every afternoon about three o'clock just like clockwork it would pour cats and dogs for about one half hour which left us drenched and trails deep in mud. However, once the sun came back out the intense heat dried us out fairly quickly. The higher we penetrated inland the harder it was to dig to find water. This was beneficial as we were able to dig our foxholes and not worry about getting our feet wet.

In early December 1943, our advance inland came to an abrupt halt. Holding us up was a fairly high hill that was dubbed "Hellzapoppin Ridge". It turned out to be a jungle fortress defended by about 250 combat veterans. Though barely 250 feet high the ridge dropped away almost sheer on both sides. The whole fortress area of about 400 yards across was matted with a wild tangle of jungle and giant size trees. At times some of our Marines got within 15 yards of the enemy where they could hear and not see them. The forward echelon of our troops was met by machine gun fire and grenades. They were lucky to get out with only a few dead and wounded. Some of our Paratroops tried a second time to reach the crest of the hill but as they struggled through the heavy cane and twisted vines they were suddenly caught in a deadly crossfire. Unfortunately they were forced to fall back but this time had to leave their dead and wounded behind. For eleven days this battle raged. The Jap defenders were very clever using stand-up foxholes which makes a man a much smaller target than the horizontal fox holes we used. Their gun pits were protected by splinter proof tops of logs and sand. They cut away roots of the huge giant trees, making hollow dugouts invulnerable to all but direct hits from mortars, artillery fire or bombs dropped from our aircraft. These giant tree tops helped to protect them from our dive bomber and strafing runs. Their whole defense system was beautifully conceived with snipers everywhere. It was stated that nine out of every ten casualties never saw the enemy.

On "Hellzapoppin" it often seemed that we were fighting blindfolded. To blast them out it took an incredible mortar, artillery and air bombardment day and night. Most of us remember how it was to be pinned to the stinking jungle earth by the sound and shock of heavy gunfire. The hard part was not knowing if and when you might become a casualty. We know what all Americans should know who have read about the sickening smell of dead Japs. Dead Americans become just as foul, blackening and bloating under the merciless sun. Not a pretty sight to see. The eleven day battle finally ended in the early evening of December 18th. Our total casualties were 158 dead or wounded. Interesting to note this battle was written up by a Marine Combat Correspondent and published in Look Magazine May 30, 1944.

One morning Xmas week 1943 we were startled as the sides of our foxholes began to fill in and the giant trees surrounding our area were dangerously swaying. We weren't sure what was happening but were later told a small earthquake had hit the island. It was a weird feeling not knowing what it was and what to do about it.

On Xmas day 1943 I was notified that I was one of ten Marines from the 3rd Marine Division selected for the Navy V-12 College Training Program. What a wonderful totally unexpected Xmas present. That Xmas night we had the worst artillery bombing of any we had and I began to wonder if I would be able to enjoy my present. However, I survived it and left aboard the U.S.S. President

Jackson to return to Guadalcanal. It was an emotional farewell to my Communication Platoon members as we had been together for over a year. All wished me the best of luck along with messages and addresses for me to write when I arrived back in the States. On January 2, 1944, I left Guadalcanal aboard the U.S.S. Matsonia the sister ship of the U.S.S. Lurline that took me to New Zealand.

The voyage back to the U.S. was quite different from our voyage to New Zealand. We were only four Marines to a stateroom. Our only duties were deck watches for four hours during daylight hours. We were stationed out on the bow of the ship watching for any sign of floating debris as well as any approaching aircraft. Near New Hebrides we ran into the tail of a typhoon and because some of the heavy waves were washing over the prow of the ship I was relieved from my watch that one day. It was quite an eerie sight as way in the distance I could see a huge spout of water. Actually typhoons in this area of the ocean seldom occur. Most of the voyage the sea was quite calm. As I spent a lot of time up on deck I saw scores of flying fish and at night I could see any fluorescent colored fish in the deep blue ocean who seemed to be following the ship. The chow on board was excellent and plentiful. I was able to spend some time in the radio room listening to and copying Morse code messages over the Fox Network. Reading, playing cards and watching a movie every night made the time pass and the voyage quite pleasant. Finally on January 20, 1944, we passed under the Golden Gate Bridge and disembarked at Treasure Island, CA. What a great feeling and relief to be back on U.S. soil.

The truck drivers who were to drive us up to temporary quarters were women Marines. Not seeing many women since leaving New Zealand, seeing them was an unexpected pleasant surprise.

On my train ride across country as we stopped in Kingman, AZ a section of the Pullman car I was in had to move to another car to make room for 12 German prisoners of war. They were being transferred to another POW camp in Prescott, AZ. Most of them carried suitcases and put them up in the overhead racks. One prisoner however, kept his in his lap. In questioning one of the armed guards he told me this fellow's suitcase was filled with various kinds of chocolate bars and he didn't want any one of his fellow prisoners stealing them from him. The trip was long and otherwise uneventful but the scenery in most every state we passed through was quite different from one another. On February 22, 1944, I arrived home in Fitchburg, MA.

During my week's furlough at home my orders came through from Headquarters Marine Corps, Washington, DC directing me to report to the Navy V-12 training program at Yale University, New Haven, CT on March 1, 1944. There I will begin sixteen months of intensive study hopefully to complete the required two years of college in order to possibly become a Marine Corps officer.

My first semester classes were General Math; History; Physics; English; Naval Law; and Engineering Drawing (Descriptive Geometry). Along with Physics and Engineering Drawing we had several hours of lab work. Being away from school for almost two years it was very difficult for me to get used to long hours of studying. Physics was especially difficult as it required knowledge of certain Math subjects like Trigonometry that I hadn't, at that time, been exposed to.

One day in May I finally received my Xmas box sent early in December 1943. It was kind of beat up and the cookies, etc. were a little stale. Non-perishables were fine. The box must have traveled about 10 to 12,000 miles before reaching me.

Starting with the second semester I had to take two periods a week of intramural sports (for outdoor conditioning). I played baseball, soccer, basketball and boxing. My biggest surprise was making the Yale varsity baseball team. I was awarded my letter "Y" and was quite satisfied with my playing not only making the baseball team but I was captain of the basketball team and won the 135 pound class boxing championship. I firmly believe my ability to play many different athletic games fairly well was instrumental in my being accepted into the Navy V-12 program as I had competed against several of the Marine officers who conducted the numerous screening boards I had to go before the final selections were made.

As I look back with fond memories of my sixteen months at Yale I remember the many long hours of studying and how difficult some of the courses were. When you have to complete two full years of college courses in a sixteen month period it wasn't an easy task. In addition we had daily drill periods as well as weekly parades. However I successfully passed all of my courses and at 0600 hours on June 29, 1945, our graduating Marines boarded a train for Camp Lejeune, North Carolina to begin our Officer Candidate training. It was an emotional farewell leaving all my roommates and many other good friends.

On July 1, 1945, I arrived at Camp Lejeune after a long and hot train ride from New Haven, Connecticut. We had a 4 hour layover in Washington, DC so to avoid the stifling heat we took in a movie where it was much cooler. It feels like "Boot Camp" all over again as discipline is really strict and the least little thing you do wrong gives you demerits. By the time all the other Marine candidates arrive we should have about 250 in our Company. We live in red brick barracks in squad bays of about 50 men each. The food is very good and plenty of it so that is a help.

On September 2, 1945, V-J Day, a Major from HQMC came down to tell us what was going to happen to us. They gave us four choices; first we could request immediate discharge regardless of service status (Regular of Reserve); second choice was to return to general duty; third was a chance to apply for Basic Training School at Quantico, VA whereupon after successfully completing six month of training we would be given a Regular commission as a 2nd Lieutenant; and fourth choice which applied to V-12 Marines only. I opted for the fourth choice which meant taking an advance course of six weeks training which would start on October 1st. Upon successfully completing the course I would be commissioned 2nd Lt. in the Marine Corps Reserve and then placed on an inactive status and discharged soon afterwards. The only catch was if I failed the course I would be sent to general duty to finish out my enlistment.

Graduation took place at 0900 hours on November 10, 1945, and I proudly became a Second Lieutenant in the United States

Marine Corps Reserve. I returned home on November 12, 1945, once again a civilian ready to start a new life.

On February 3, 1974, I retired from the U.S. Marines as a Lieutenant Colonel, USMCR.

Ed and Priscilla Clough
January 1999, Married 53 years

Author's Note:

The end of a journey is determined in advance by the direction one chooses to travel. We owe such a debt of gratitude to all veterans who proudly served this great country. Through their efforts as part of their life's journey, we are all privileged to share in this great democracy. They are men and women of strong character.

CONCLUSION

Through the first 50 years of the Twentieth Century our parents and grandparents never lost sight of their dream for the promise of a better life. They accomplished this through individual progress and self- determination. They made the most out of the life they lived. Much of their happiness was found by doing acts of kindness and showing justice to neighbors and friends. Respect and responsibility were considered virtues with true meaning. During the turmoil of the 1930's the lifestyle of our parents was reflected by the worst economic time our country has ever been through. During the 1940's our families lived through a time in which they experienced the horror and devastation of the world's worst war. As the war raged on brothers, fathers, uncles and sisters stood tall and went off to battle. It was through their heroism and devotion in standing up for truth and righteousness that enabled us to have the freedom that we enjoy today.

We live in the present, the future is a dream, but the past is a fact. As we enter into the 21st Millennium it seems only fitting and proper to pause and reflect on the lives and lifestyles of our parents and grandparents. This is where we gain an appreciation and an understanding of the very special gift we have inherited from them:

The right to seek happiness and success.

 Bill Thomson is a native New Englander residing in Kennebunk Maine. Retired Professor Emeritus from Salem State College, Salem Massachusetts. He has written 20 books and produced 7 documentaries which have been shown on New England television channels. He has also appeared on National P.B.S., the Learning Channel and the Discovery Channel.

MAJOR NEWS EVENTS

1900 - 1950
Thousands of news events occurred in the 50 years between 1900 and 1950 and each one was significant, meaningful and had an impact on life. The following are a few of these events.

1900
January 1st - On this date the new century was rung in with great enthusiasm. The population was optimistic as it seemed the 20th century would be full of promise and self satisfaction. The economy was good.

October 30th - The population of the United States reached 76,295,220 people. This was a 20% gain since the last census in 1890.

November 6th - President William McKinley won re-election. His Vice President was the former Governor of New York and famed Rough Rider, Theodore Roosevelt.

1901
September 14th - President McKinley was assassinated. Vice President Theodore Roosevelt was sworn in as America's 26th president.

1906
April 19th - San Francisco, California was in flames and reduced to rubble after a major earthquake. Over 1,000 people died.

1912
January 12th - Mill workers in Lawrence, Mass. went on strike for more money. They were receiving 16 cents an hour or about $8.00 per week for 50 to 60 hours of work. The strike lasted 9 weeks reaching violent proportions as mill machinery and

property were smashed. The militia was called out and some deaths occurred.

April 15th - The Titanic sank and 1,595 people drowned.

1913
October 10th - President Wilson pushed a button that ignited a dynamite explosion that opened the last section of the Panama Canal. The Atlantic and Pacific oceans were now joined.

1914
June 28th - Archduke Franz Ferdinard, the heir to the Austrian-Hungary throne was assassinated. This marked the beginning of World War I.

1917
April 6th - The United States entered World War I. President Wilson signed the Declaration of War against Germany as he proclaimed that the world must be made safe for democracy.

1918
October 31st - An influenza epidemic killed as many as 20 million people throughout the world.

November 11th - World War I ended when Germany signed an armistice.

1920
January 16th - Prohibition went into effect. Beer, wine and liquor were banned by the 18th amendment.

August 26th - American women were granted voting rights by passage of The 19th Amendment.

1927

May 21st - Lindbergh flew across the Atlantic ocean, non-stop from New York to Paris.

1929

October 24th - The stock market crashed. Billions of dollars were lost. The depression followed.

1930

October 23rd - President Hoover announced plans to combat the depression.

1932

November 8th - Franklin D. Roosevelt won a landslide victory for President of the United States.

1933

December 5th - Prohibition came to an end. The 18th amendment was repealed.

1938

January 1st - Eight million Americans were jobless. At least 20% of workforce unemployed.

1941

December 7th 7:59 a.m. the Japanese bombed Pearl Harbor in a surprise attack. Over 2,000 Americans died and hundreds more were wounded.

December 8th - United States declared war on Japan

December 11th - United States declared war on Italy and Germany

1943

October 13th - Italy surrendered and declared war on Germany.

1945

April 12th - President Roosevelt died and Vice President Truman assumed the presidency.

May 7th - Germany unconditionally surrendered.

August 6th - Hiroshima, Japan was destroyed by an atomic bomb dropped by the United States - 60% of the city was wiped out. The atomic age had begun.

August 9th - Nagasaki, Japan was leveled with a second atomic bomb dropped by the United States - 30% of the city's industrial area was destroyed.

August 10th - Japan offered to surrender.

September 2nd - Japan unconditionally surrendered.   Peace documents were signed aboard the battleship Missouri.

Note: In 1945 when World War II ended, 50 million people worldwide had lost their lives. Of these, 17 million men and women died in the service of their country and over 33 million civilians were killed through war related activities. 292,000 young American veterans would never return and over 1.7 million more were injured. This was the worst war in history. Germany was in ruins, and many European countries had been reduced to rubble. The United States temporarily controlled Japanese territory. Parts of Europe, Asia and Africa faced starvation. The Soviet Union and the United States emerged as the two greatest world powers.

1949

September 23rd - The Russians developed an atomic bomb

October 1st - The Peoples Republic was established in China and China became a Communist nation.

Bibliography

The Big Change, America Transforms Itself 1900-1950
(Harper, NY) 1952 by Frederick Lewis Allen

The Fabulous Century 1940-1950 Time Life Books

America Remembers The Home Front by Roy Hoopes

Don't You Know There's A War On? (G.P. Putnam's NY) 1940
by Richard Lingeman

Granmma Remembers New England by William O. Thomson

Grampa Remembers Unusual Happenings in Old New England
by William O. Thomson

Special thanks to additional contributors

Tom and Jean Bridges
Nancy Chase
Donald and Betty Matthews
John and Ginny Matthews
Doris McGlynn
Andrew Thomson

Cover Painting by Ron Goyette

Ron's studio is in Kennebunkport Maine. He is ranked as one of
New England's most esteemed artists. His ability to capture the
moods of land, sea, lighthouses, ships and harbors have brought
him national acclaim. He is a master in turn of the century scenes
and his work is in great demand.

Children

If there is anything I love to see,
It's a bunch of children around me.
Knowing that time is mine
To play and let my thoughts incline.

Roll on the floor with youngsters fine,
Get better acquainted all the time -
With those who soon will be,
Grown up dreamers, just like me.

They help us to forget petty strife,
Make us long for a larger life -
Urging us on to a goal worthwhile
Loving and serving with a smile.

November 30, 1930

William Thomson Sr.
1873 - 1956